LIGHT and STYLISH

SOUTH AFRICAN MEALS WITH A DIFFERENCE

Pat Barton * Magdaleen van Wyk
Photographs by Alain Proust

Struik Publishers

About the authors

MAGDALEEN VAN WYK is a lecturer in the Department of Home Economics at Stellenbosch University and has written a number of cookery books, including *The Complete South African Cookbook*, *South African Fruit Cooking and Preserving* and *Cooking the South African Way*.

PAT BARTON is a freelance editor. She has edited, and collaborated on, many cookery books and is the compiler of *The Complete South African Kilojoule, Calorie and Carbohydrate Counter*.

Thanks are due to the following for supplying accessories:
Binnehuis Interiors (Pty) Ltd – porcelain
Fountain Framers (Pty) Ltd – ceramics
The House Shop, Boardmans – perspex

Front cover: **Smoked salmon and shrimp parcels**
Title page: **Melon with pecan nuts**
Contents page: **Lemon granite**

Struik Publishers
An operating division of
Struik Holdings (Pty) Ltd
Struik House
Oswald Pirow Street
Cape Town 8001

Registration no.: 80/02842/07

First published 1988

Text © Magdaleen van Wyk and Pat Barton 1988
Photographs © Struik Publishers 1988

House editor Kate McCallum
Designer Janice Evans
Cover designer Abdul Amien

Typesetting by Diatype Setting cc, Cape Town
Reproduction by Unifoto (Pty) Ltd, Cape Town
Printed and bound by CTP Book Printers, Parow

ISBN 0 86977 385 2

METRIC CONVERSIONS USED IN THIS BOOK

Volume

¼ teaspoon	=	1 ml
½ teaspoon	=	2 ml
1 teaspoon	=	5 ml
1½ teaspoons	=	7 ml
2 teaspoons	=	10 ml
3 teaspoons	=	15 ml
4 teaspoons	=	20 ml
1 tablespoon	=	15 ml
2 tablespoons	=	30 ml
3 tablespoons	=	45 ml
4 tablespoons	=	60 ml
¼ cup	=	65 ml
½ cup	=	125 ml
¾ cup	=	200 ml
1 cup	=	250 ml
1½ cups	=	375 ml
2 cups	=	500 ml
3 cups	=	750 ml

Mass

1 oz	=	30 g
¼ lb	=	125 g
½ lb	=	250 g
1 lb	=	500 g
2 lbs	=	1 kg

Gram equivalents of 250 ml

Butter/margarine	230 g
Cheese, grated	100 g
Cheese, cottage or cream	250 g
Flour, bread/cake	120 g
self-raising	140 g
wholewheat	130 g
Nuts, chopped	150 g
Rice, uncooked	200 g
Sugar, granulated	200 g
castor	210 g
icing	130 g

CONTENTS

GLOSSARY

amandine
A dish having almonds as a major ingredient.

anchoiade
A savoury mixture, based on anchovies, which is used either as a butter or as a dip, depending on the consistency.

baby mealies
Immature mealie cobs, which are delicious steamed and served as a vegetable, in salads or braaied. They also make a delicate addition to stir-fried dishes.

banana peppers
Smallish yellow or orange peppers with an elongated shape and a mild sweet flavour. They are delicious in salads and stir-fried dishes.

bombe
A moulded ice cream, originally made in a round mould (hence the name), usually with a firm outer wall of ice cream and a mixture of ingredients in the centre. It is turned out of the mould for serving.

Calvados
A liqueur made from apples.

charlotte mould
A special ridged mould used for hot or cold main courses or desserts that are served turned out onto a platter. The resulting dish is called a charlotte.

cheeses
A number of varieties of the strong-flavoured *Cheddar cheese* are available locally, ranging from a milder, soft consistency cheese to a fairly hard matured cheese. Cheddar is the preferred cheese for toppings that are to be grilled. *Drakensberg* is a soft, full-fat orange cheese, manufactured locally. It has a creamy texture and a fairly strong flavour. It's primarily an eating cheese, but is good in salads, too. *Feta cheese* is a salty white Greek cheese traditionally made from ewe's or goat's milk, and is available in this country made either from goat's or cow's milk. It is superb in green salads or in stir-fried dishes. A sweet, nutty pale yellow cheese with characteristic holes, *Gruyère* is generally used in fondues and sauces, but goes equally well in salads. *Mozzarella cheese* is a soft, full-fat white Italian cheese that goes particularly well with tomatoes. It is often used as the cheese base for pizzas. A hard, granular cheese, *Parmesan cheese*, when fully matured, is used grated as a garnish for salads, in pasta dishes and in pizzas. *Ricotta cheese* is a soft, unripened cheese made from the whey of cow's milk. It is

smooth and mild-tasting, and is used in a variety of sweet and savoury dishes, including pizzas. *Rosetta cheese* is a locally manufactured soft, full-fat cheese, orange in colour, with a tangy flavour. An excellent eating cheese, it goes well with fruit and is good in salads. *Cottage cheese* is a mild-tasting curd cheese with a moist texture. It is available either smooth or chunky and often with flavourings like chives and onions added. It's extremely versatile and is used in dishes as varied as cheesecake, pastry, salads and baked dishes. Cottage cheese is the dieter's wonder cheese because of its versatility and because it contains far fewer kilojoules than most hard cheeses.

Chinese cabbage
Also called Chinese leaves. A leafy cabbage with a long head, the leaves are more like a firm lettuce than the familiar cabbage. Used in salads and stir-fried dishes.

clarified butter
Butter which has been boiled and strained through a very thin sieve lined with thin muslin or filter paper to remove impurities. Refrigerate clear liquid for up to six weeks.

corniottes
Savoury individual pies shaped like raised Cornish pasties.

couscous
A cereal, made from semolina, which forms the main ingredient in a spicy North African stew of the same name.

crudités
Strips, chunks or other shaped pieces of crisp raw vegetables, served with dips. Popular ingredients include mushrooms, green pepper, cherry tomatoes, celery stalks, cauliflower florets, spring onions and cucumber slices.

cucumber
In addition to the short knobbly variety, there are two others which are popular, particularly in salads. *English cucumbers* are long knobbly cucumbers with a sweet flavour, generally used with the skin. *American sweetslice cucumbers* are large smooth-skinned cucumbers with a sweet flavour.

fettuccini
Also called tagliatelli. A fairly broad ribbon noodle pasta which may be white or green (with spinach added).

fish roe
The eggs of fish such as snoek, which is fried or grilled. *Caviar*, the roe of the sturgeon, is

exorbitantly expensive in this country and *Danish lumpfish roe* is often used as a substitute.

gnocchi
Savoury balls, often made with spinach or potatoes, cooked in barely simmering water until just tender and served with grated Parmesan cheese.

haarder
A small bony fish which is excellent grilled or smoked. It is also available dried, when it is called a *bokkom*.

julienne
To cut into thin matchstick strips. Generally used for vegetables to be served in a salad, steamed or used in stir-fried dishes.

kiwi fruit
Also called Chinese gooseberry. A green-fleshed fruit with a circle of tiny black seeds around the core, kiwi fruit has a slightly sour taste and is used in purées, fruit salads, whips and dessert mousses.

lettuce
Many varieties of lettuce are now available. The firm-head *iceberg lettuce* is crisp with whitish green leaves. *Cos lettuce* has a long firm head with crisp whitish green leaves. The green-leafed *butter lettuce* is softer and sweeter in flavour and ideal for use in salads. *Oak lettuce*, which has soft green leaves tinged at the tips with red, is a new salad favourite, while the *Baby Gem lettuce* – small with firm light green leaves – has a sweet delicate flavour.

macerate
To soak fruit in a sweet marinade, wine or spirits.

mangetout
Also called snow peas and (some varieties) sugar snap peas. Early varieties of peas with very tender pods, they need only to be topped and tailed before steaming or eating raw. Popular salad ingredients and also used in stir-fried dishes.

mezes
The Greek name for appetizers.

mineolas
Soft-skinned citrus fruit with a very juicy bright orange flesh, somewhere between an orange and a naartjie in size and flavour.

mushrooms
Button mushrooms are small and white.

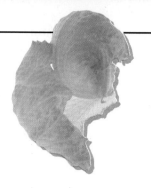

Brown mushrooms are larger, with a more intense flavour. *Oyster mushrooms* are smallish flat white mushrooms with a delicate flavour, ideal in salads.

mustard
Many varieties of prepared mustards are available. *Dijon mustard* is a mild, sweet-flavoured mustard, *French mustard* also has a mild flavour and *English mustard* is very hot and spicy. *Wholegrain mustard* has whole or coarsely ground mustard seeds in it.

Ogen melon
A soft-skinned, sweet, green-fleshed melon.

oil
A number of varieties are available. *Olive oil*, pressed from olives, is a strong-flavoured oil best used with robust dishes and in salad dressings. *Sunflower* or *vegetable oil* is the most commonly used oil for cooking in this country. *Sesame oil* is the oil pressed from sesame seeds, which adds a piquant flavour to salad dressings and stir-fried dishes.

orzo
Small, rice-shaped pasta, often used in salads.

papinos
Smallish, very intensely orange-coloured pawpaws with a strong sweet flavour.

parfait
A layered cold dessert made and served in tall glasses.

pasty
Individual savoury pies which have the pastry edges gathered up and pressed together over the filling for a raised effect.

persimmons
Also called Kaki fruit. A soft, fleshy pale orange fruit which is eaten raw or used in cooking, and is often glacéed.

pesto
The classic pesto consists of very finely chopped basil pounded with pine kernels and oil to make a savoury and quite stiff sauce. Other herbs, such as coriander and parsley, may be used instead of basil.

pine kernels
The fruit of the pine. The small elongated kernels have a delicately sweet flavour.

potted
Used to describe a dish in which fish, seafood or cheese is finely shredded and pressed into small containers before chilling.

praline
A mixture of very finely chopped nuts and sugar syrup, which is allowed to harden and is then crushed and served over desserts.

radish
Many varieties of radish are available. White radishes are longer and much milder than red ones.

raita
A mixture of vegetables (and sometimes fruit), rather like sambals, which is generally served as a condiment with curried or spicy dishes.

ramekin
A small ovenproof dish used to cook individual baked dishes.

risotto
A baked savoury dish with meat, fish or poultry and vegetables, or vegetables on their own, added.

roulade
A kind of swiss roll, made of a sponge mixture or pastry, with a savoury filling.

roux
A mixture of heated butter and flour, which forms the base of white or brown sauces.

saté
Meat, generally pork, or poultry threaded onto skewers and grilled.

spaghettini
Very thin pasta noodles, used primarily for deep-frying.

swiss chard
Also called chard. Similar in appearance and taste to spinach, but with a milder flavour.

tahini
A paste made from ground sesame seeds, which goes particularly well with garlic, lemon juice, soy sauce, yoghurt, buttermilk, orange juice and fresh herbs to make dressings and sauces. It's available canned but you can make it yourself by grinding sesame seeds in a coffee grinder or food processor and mixing them with French dressing.

terrine
Baked layered pâté which may consist of meat or fish with vegetable layers or of vegetables only.

timbales
Small conical moulded savoury mixtures baked in the oven and turned out to serve.

tuiles
Paper-thin butter biscuits, often served as an accompaniment to desserts.

tulipes
Very thin biscuits shaped into tulip-shaped 'baskets' by placing them over an inverted container while still hot, and leaving them to cool. They are used as containers for ice cream or fruity desserts.

vinaigrette
A salad dressing of vinegar and oil, also called French dressing. Various other flavourings – including garlic, herbs, mustard and curry – may be added.

vinegar
Vinegar is available in many varieties. *Grape vinegar*, the most commonly used, is distilled from grapes and can be white or brown. *Wine vinegar*, both white and red, is distilled from wine and is much more delicate in flavour. *Cider vinegar* is made from apples and has a very strong flavour. In cooking, it is used primarily when apples are an ingredient. *Tarragon vinegar* is one of the many flavoured vinegars on the market. Others include rosemary, raspberry and thyme vinegar.

water chestnuts
A tuber cultivated in the East, which is used sliced as a vegetable and is usually bought canned outside of Asia. It adds a crunchy flavour to salads and stir-fried dishes.

watercress
A small-leafed plant with a pungent taste, which is used as a salad green or as a garnish. It is also often puréed, raw, and used in vegetable terrines.

yeast
Active yeast consists of dried granules, which must be rehydrated with the liquid in the recipe before use. *Instant yeast* consists of dried granules which can be used instantly and do not require rehydrating. Using instant yeast cuts rising time by half, but once the packet is opened the yeast cannot be stored.

yoghurt
Yoghurt, usually made from whole milk, is also made from skimmed milk (low-fat yoghurt). Yoghurt without any flavouring added is generally unsweetened and is referred to as *natural* or *plain yoghurt*, or as *Bulgarian yoghurt*. Yoghurt to which flavourings have been added may be full-fat or low-fat, and usually has sweetening added. *Drinking yoghurt* is natural yoghurt of a pouring consistency.

BREAKFASTS

et off to a good start with a breakfast that's satisfying and well-balanced nutritionally, but not too heavy. For workers in a hurry, the **Working person's breakfast** menu will be a boon. Slimmers can try the high-energy breakfast in a glass – **Energy whip** is a quick and easy way to ensure balanced low-kilojoule nutrition. If you prefer an **English breakfast**, our menu is an interesting variation on traditional bacon and eggs. The **Wedding brunch** menu is simple to prepare, yet looks and tastes spectacular; it's ideal for any special occasion.

Clockwise from top: **Wholewheat cheese toasts with sesame seeds, fresh pawpaw and granadilla juice, fruit muesli with yoghurt**

Working person's breakfast

(Menu for 4)

Fresh pawpaw and granadilla juice

Fruit muesli with yoghurt

Wholewheat cheese toasts with sesame seeds

OR

Energy whip

Rosehip tea

Fresh pawpaw and granadilla juice

½ large ripe pawpaw, peeled and seeded
125 ml fresh orange juice
6 ripe granadillas

Chop pawpaw flesh coarsely and mix with orange juice. Remove pulp from granadillas and add to pawpaw. Whisk fruit in a blender or food processor and serve chilled.
Serves 4

Note
● *The pawpaw and granadilla juice may be blended the evening before and stored in the refrigerator until needed.*

Fruit muesli with yoghurt

500 ml muesli *
chopped fresh fruit of your choice
500 ml natural yoghurt
honey (optional)

Spoon muesli into individual bowls. Top with fresh fruit and pour yoghurt over. Top with honey to taste, and serve.
Serves 4

Notes
● *Chop the fruit the evening before, mix with yoghurt and store in the refrigerator. To serve, mix with muesli and top with honey.*
● *For slimmers, serve muesli with skim milk or fruit juice only.*

Muesli

125 ml dried apples
125 ml dried apricots
500 ml rolled oats
250 ml wheat flakes
30 ml wheat germ
65 ml digestive bran
125 ml seedless raisins or sultanas
125 ml chopped mixed nuts
125 ml skimmed milk powder

Chop dried apples and apricots finely. Combine with remaining ingredients and store in an airtight container until needed.
Makes 1,5 litres

Wholewheat cheese toasts with sesame seeds

4 thin slices wholewheat bread, toasted and buttered
100 ml grated Cheddar cheese
50 ml toasted sesame seeds

Topping
30 ml butter or margarine
60 ml cake flour
125 ml milk
5 ml prepared French mustard
15 ml Worcestershire sauce
salt and freshly ground black pepper
500 ml grated Cheddar cheese

First make topping. Melt butter or margarine in a saucepan over low heat. Add flour and cook, stirring, for 2-3 minutes. Adding milk gradually, stir until smooth and thick. Add remaining ingredients and cook, stirring, until cheese melts. Spread topping on buttered wholewheat toast, top with 100 ml grated Cheddar cheese and sesame seeds and grill until topping is golden and bubbling. Serve immediately.
Serves 4

Notes
● *The cheese topping will keep for up to 1 week in the refrigerator. It is not suitable for freezing.*
● *Toast sesame seeds on a baking sheet in the oven at 160 °C until golden, or heat a little oil in a frying pan, add sesame seeds and toast, stirring, until golden.*

Energy whip

250 ml low-fat buttermilk
1 ripe banana, peeled and chopped
65 ml wheat germ
10 ml honey
75 ml chopped fresh fruit of your choice

Place all ingredients in a food processor or blender and blend until smooth. Pour into a tall glass and serve.
Serves 1

Notes
● *Low-fat natural yoghurt may be used instead of buttermilk.*
● *Chopped fresh pears or grated tart apples go particularly well with the banana.*
● *For a slightly spicier taste, add a shake of ground nutmeg and ground ginger or cinnamon before blending the ingredients.*
● *Add freshly squeezed orange juice, or fruit juice of your choice, for a runnier consistency.*
● *Serve this to slimmers instead of fruit muesli * and wholewheat cheese toasts *.*

Rosehip tea
Allow 1 sachet rosehip tea per person. Steep in boiling water to strength required and serve, sweetened with honey. Rosehip tea* sachets are available from health stores and some supermarkets.

Grilled grapefruit (top), eggs Benedict and grilled bacon, pâté-stuffed mushrooms, grilled peppered mackerel (left front)

English breakfast

(Menu for 4)

Grilled grapefruit

Grilled peppered mackerel

Eggs Benedict and grilled bacon

Pâté-stuffed mushrooms

Muffins

Tea   Coffee

Grilled peppered mackerel

4 peppered mackerel fillets
20 ml butter

Place mackerel fillets in a grilling pan and dot each with butter. Grill for about 2 minutes on each side, or until cooked through. Serve with grilled bacon*, eggs Benedict* and pâté-stuffed mushrooms.*
Serves 4

Note
• *Mackerel fillets may also be heated in the microwave oven.*

Grilled grapefruit

2 large rosé grapefruit, halved
15 ml butter
30 ml brown sugar
2 ml ground cinnamon

Loosen grapefruit segments from core and rind to make them easy to remove. Spread butter over grapefruit halves and sprinkle each with sugar mixed with cinnamon. Grill until topping is hot and bubbling (about 4 minutes) and serve.
Serves 4

Eggs Benedict

4 eggs
2 muffins*, brioches or soft rolls, halved
butter
salt and freshly ground pepper

Hollandaise sauce
4 egg yolks
20 ml lukewarm water
250 g butter
150 ml boiling water
salt and freshly ground pepper
15 ml fresh lemon juice

Poach eggs in a poaching pan over boiling water until done to taste. Meanwhile, make hollandaise sauce. Whisk egg yolks with lukewarm water in top of a double boiler. Place over simmering water and add butter, a little at a time, whisking constantly. Do not allow to boil. Gradually add boiling water, still whisking, and season with salt and pepper to taste and lemon juice. Whisk until well-combined. Do not allow to boil again, as sauce will curdle if it becomes too hot. Toast muffin, brioche or roll halves and butter them. Place a poached egg on each half, season to taste with salt and pepper and top with hot hollandaise sauce.
Serves 4

Grilled bacon
Allow 2-3 rashers per person. Snip off rinds and grill until done to taste. Bacon should be well cooked but not too crisp.

Pâté-stuffed mushrooms

4 large brown mushroom caps
salt and freshly ground black pepper
50 ml dried breadcrumbs
20 ml very finely chopped parsley
20 ml butter

Chicken liver pâté
200 g butter, margarine or sunflower oil
500 g chicken livers
250 g mushrooms, finely chopped
1 large green pepper, seeded and finely chopped
1 small onion, finely chopped
125 ml dry white wine or sherry
1 clove garlic, crushed
1 ml dill seeds
5 ml salt
4 drops hot pepper sauce

First make pâté. Heat 65 ml butter, margarine or oil in a frying pan and sauté liver, mushrooms, green pepper and onion for 5 minutes. Add wine or sherry, garlic, dill seeds, salt and hot pepper sauce and simmer, covered, until livers and mushrooms are very tender (about 10 minutes). Remove from stove. Cool mixture slightly, then blend with remaining butter, margarine or oil in a blender or food processor until smooth. Pack tightly in an earthenware crock and chill for at least 3 hours before serving. (Makes 750 ml)
Wipe mushroom caps well, and season with salt and pepper. Fill cavities with 50 ml chicken liver pâté. Combine breadcrumbs with parsley, sprinkle over mushrooms and dot with butter. Grill until mushrooms are cooked through and topping is golden and bubbling (about 8 minutes). Serve hot.
Serves 4

Note
• *Serve the leftover chicken liver pâté with fresh wholewheat bread or Melba toast* as a starter. It can be frozen, too.*

Muffins

200 ml wholewheat flour
250 ml cake flour
25 ml baking powder
2 ml salt
125 ml milk
1 egg, well-beaten
75 ml sunflower oil
65 ml honey

Stir wholewheat flour, cake flour, baking powder and salt together in a mixing bowl. Combine milk, egg, oil and honey and add to dry ingredients. Stir until just moistened. Fill greased muffin pans to ⅔ full and bake in a pre-heated oven at 200°C for 20 minutes, or until golden brown.
Makes 12

Note
• *Muffins will keep for up to 1 week in an airtight container or in the freezer for up to 1 month.*

Wedding brunch

(Menu for 12-14)

Frittata

Brioches with
fruity nut cheese

Whole baked fish with a salt crust

Tangy curry dressing

Blue cheese dressing

Fennel dressing

Green salad with apple dressing

Fresh fruit bowl

Frozen Amarula bombe with berry purée

Buck's fizz

Kir

Coffee

Frittata

12 large eggs, lightly beaten
500 ml diced cooked ham
500 ml grated mature Cheddar or Drakensberg cheese
125 ml coarsely chopped parsley
salt and freshly ground pepper
45 ml butter

In a large bowl stir together eggs, half the ham, cheese and parsley. Season to taste. Melt butter in a large non-stick frying pan and pour in egg mixture. Cook, without stirring, for 12-14 minutes, or until eggs are almost set. Sprinkle with remaining ham, cheese and parsley and cook, covered with foil, for 1-2 minutes or until just set. Serve cut into wedges.
Serves 12-14

From left: Apple dressing, sour cream with chives, green salad, brioches.

Fruity nut cheese

500 g chunky cottage cheese
100 ml cream
100 ml sultanas
100 ml chopped soaked dried fruits
100 ml chopped blanched almonds

Combine all ingredients well and spoon into a serving dish. Chill until ready to serve. Serve with brioches.
Serves 12-14

Notes

• *Soak chopped dried fruit of your choice in water, fruit juice or brandy until plump (at least 1 hour).*
• *The fruity nut cheese may be prepared the previous evening.*

Whole baked fish with a salt crust

2 whole white steenbras, gutted
100 ml chopped fresh dill
2 kg coarse salt

Stuff each fish with 50 ml chopped dill. Coat fish with a 5 mm thick layer of coarse salt, pressing salt onto fish firmly with your hands. Place fish in large baking pans and bake in a pre-heated oven at 180°C for 45-60 minutes, depending on size of fish. Place baked fish on a platter. Break open salt crust and serve immediately with tangy curry dressing*, blue cheese dressing*, and fennel dressing*.
Serves 12-14

Tangy curry dressing

4 rashers bacon, crisply fried and crumbled
250 g smooth cottage cheese
45 ml milk
50 ml olive oil
30 ml fresh lemon juice
10 ml curry powder
2 ml ground cumin
65 ml fruit chutney
1 ml Tabasco sauce
salt

Blend bacon, cheese, milk, oil, lemon juice, curry powder, cumin and chutney in a blender or food processor until smooth. Add Tabasco sauce and salt to taste.
Makes about 375 ml

Blue cheese dressing

125 ml crumbled Blaauwkranz cheese
375 ml sour cream or natural yoghurt
65 ml milk
30 ml mayonnaise
15 ml olive oil
30 ml white wine vinegar
2 ml paprika
salt

Blend cheese, sour cream or yoghurt, milk, mayonnaise, oil and vinegar in a blender or food processor until smooth. Add paprika and salt to taste.
Makes about 550 ml

Fennel dressing

250 g smooth cottage cheese
125 ml natural yoghurt
125 ml loosely packed fresh parsley leaves
125 ml loosely packed fresh fennel sprigs, trimmed
125 ml chopped spring onion ($\pm$5 spring onions)
15 ml white wine vinegar
65 ml sunflower oil
10 ml Worcestershire sauce
30 ml milk
salt and freshly ground black pepper

Blend cottage cheese, yoghurt, parsley, fennel and spring onion in a blender or food processor until smooth. With motor running, add vinegar, oil, Worcestershire sauce, milk, and salt and pepper to taste. Blend until well-combined.
Makes about 500 ml

Note
• *The dressings can be prepared the evening before and stored in the refrigerator until needed.*

From top: **Tangy curry dressing, blue cheese dressing, fennel dressing**

Green salad with apple dressing

300 g watercress, trimmed
1 small oak lettuce, separated into leaves
1 small cos lettuce or red butter lettuce, separated into leaves
1 small butter lettuce, separated into leaves
10 young spinach leaves or curly endive leaves
1 head chicory, broken into leaves
50 ml toasted and chopped hazelnuts or quail's eggs for garnish
snipped fresh chives for garnish

Apple dressing
1 medium onion, very finely chopped
1 clove garlic, crushed
15 ml white wine vinegar
salt and freshly ground pepper
100 ml olive or sunflower oil
1 large Granny Smith apple, cored and chopped

Combine dressing ingredients in a blender or food processor until well-blended. Arrange watercress, lettuces, spinach and chicory in a large salad bowl. Top with nuts or quail's eggs and chives. Serve with apple dressing or sour cream and chives.
Serves 12-14

Fruit bowl
Pile ripe fruit in a glass bowl and garnish with mint.
Buck's fizz
Combine 1,5 litres fresh orange juice with 2 x 750 ml bottles sparkling wine. Serve chilled, in glasses, with ice-cubes.
Kir
Dip rims of 12-14 champagne glasses in a little crème de cassis, let excess drip off, and dip rims in sugar. Pour 10 ml crème de cassis into each glass and top up with chilled sparkling wine.

Frozen Amarula bombe with berry purée

Bombe
375 ml sugar
6 eggs at room temperature
6 egg yolks at room temperature
45 ml Amarula liqueur
750 ml whipping cream

Berry purée
300 g strawberries, youngberries or loganberries
sugar to taste
20 ml Amarula liqueur

First make bombe. Place sugar, eggs and yolks in the top of a double-boiler over warm water and beat over low heat for 10-12 minutes, or until thick and creamy. Transfer egg mixture to a mixer or food processor and beat until stiff (about 10 minutes). Blend in Amarula liqueur. Whip cream in a large bowl until soft peaks form. Fold gently into egg mixture, blending well, and pour into a 1,5 litre mould, rinsed with water or sprayed with non-stick cooking spray. Freeze until firm and set (about 5 hours or overnight).

To make berry purée, blend all ingredients in a food processor or blender until smooth. Turn bombe out onto a chilled plate and serve with berry purée poured over and around it.
Serves 6-8

Notes
● *To serve 12-14, make 2 frozen Amarula bombes and double the quantity of berry purée.*
● *Purée the berries the evening before and store in the refrigerator until needed. The bombe may also be prepared in advance and stored in the freezer until needed.*

Frozen Amarula bombe with berry purée

ALFRESCO MEALS

*E*ating out of doors is a popular South African pastime, but it needn't be limited to summertime treats or the traditional meat braai. Fish is delicious cooked over the coals, especially when accompanied by the delicate flavours of the grilled vegetables on the **Fish braai** menu; it's a meal that can be enjoyed all year round. The **Poolside buffet** menu is perfect for a balmy day in spring, when young fresh vegetables are at their best, or for a mild autumn evening. Return to the leisureliness of bygone days with our **Picnic** menu – an old-fashioned idea brought right up to date with imaginative pack-and-carry delights. For a taste that's really different, try the **Tandoori chicken grill** menu or the delightful mixture of flavours on the **Middle Eastern mezes** menu. And as a grand finale, the **Mexican braai** menu will tempt the tastebuds with the tanginess of Mexican foods adapted to suit local palates.

Fish braai

(Menu for 4)

Grilled yellow fin tuna steaks

Mussel and perlemoen bake

Grilled brinjals

Grilled mealie cobs in herbed mustard butter

Potato salad with green pea mayonnaise

Marinated spinach salad

Baby marrow and carrot cake

Chilled white wine, vinho verde or blanc de noir

Grilled yellow fin tuna steaks

4 yellow fin tuna steaks, each 200-250 g
lemon wedges for garnish

Marinade
50 ml melted butter
50 ml sunflower oil
10 ml fresh lemon juice
5 ml chopped fresh fennel
5 ml chopped fresh oregano
5 ml salt

Combine marinade ingredients and marinate tuna steaks in it for at least 2 hours. Remove tuna and reserve marinade. Braai tuna quickly on both sides over hot coals, then raise grid and braai over medium coals until cooked through (about 10-15 minutes), basting often with reserved marinade. Serve immediately with lemon wedges.
Serves 4

Note
● *Do not cook the tuna for too long, as it becomes tough and dry. To test, insert a skewer when fish becomes opaque – it should still look moist.*

Mussel and perlemoen bake

5 ml sunflower oil
1 clove garlic, crushed
1 onion, sliced
1 perlemoen, cleaned, pounded and sliced
18 black mussels, cleaned
1 green pepper, seeded and sliced
1 large ripe tomato, skinned and chopped
5 ml salt
5 ml chopped fresh oregano
1 bay leaf
5 ml fresh lemon juice
125 ml dry white wine

Heat oil in a cast iron pot and sauté garlic and onion until onion is transparent (about 5 minutes). Add remaining ingredients and simmer, covered, over braai fire for 30 minutes, or until mussels and perlemoen are tender.
Serves 4

Grilled brinjals
Place 4 small brinjals on the edge of the grid, over the cooler part of the braai. Cook, turning frequently, for 30-40 minutes.

From left: **Marinated spinach salad,**
mussel and perlemoen bake,
grilled yellow fin tuna steaks,
grilled mealie cobs in herbed
mustard butter,
grilled brinjals

Grilled mealie cobs in herbed mustard butter

4 mealie cobs in husks

Herbed mustard butter
5 ml prepared French mustard
100 g butter, softened
10 ml finely chopped fresh parsley
5 ml finely chopped fresh chives
5 ml finely chopped spring onion
5 ml fresh lemon juice
2 ml salt
freshly ground black pepper

First make herbed mustard butter. Combine all ingredients and chill for at least 1 hour.

Peel back, but do not remove, corn husks. Remove silky threads. Soak cobs and husks in water for 10 minutes. Spread half the herbed mustard butter on cobs and fold husks back over cobs. Wrap each in foil and braai over hot coals for 15-20 minutes, turning often. To serve, remove foil from cobs, peel off husks and serve with remaining herbed mustard butter.
Serves 4

Note
● *The herbed mustard butter may be prepared the day before.*

Potato salad with green pea mayonnaise

1 kg small new potatoes

Green pea mayonnaise
250 ml fresh young peas or frozen peas, steamed
125 ml natural yoghurt
125 ml mayonnaise
2 cloves garlic, crushed
30 ml chopped fresh chives
30 ml chopped fresh mint
salt and freshly ground black pepper

Boil potatoes in their jackets in salted water until just tender (10-15 minutes). Drain and set aside until cool enough to handle, then skin potatoes.

To make mayonnaise, purée peas with yoghurt, mayonnaise and garlic, fold in herbs and season. Pour over still hot potatoes.
Serves 4

Notes
● *If larger potatoes are used, slice them before pouring the dressing over.*
● *If preferred, pea purée may be pressed through a sieve to remove the skins.*

Potato salad with green pea mayonnaise

Baby marrow and carrot cake

Marinated spinach salad

500 g young spinach
100 g black olives
100 g feta cheese, cubed
1 onion, sliced
125 ml pine kernels

Marinade
50 ml sunflower oil
10 ml fresh lemon juice
10 ml chopped fresh basil
5 ml chopped fresh thyme
salt and freshly ground black pepper

First make marinade. Combine and shake all ingredients in a screw-top jar until well-blended.

Steam spinach lightly. Roll leaves up loosely into small parcels and pour marinade over. Marinate for 1 hour. Sprinkle olives, cheese, onion and pine kernels over spinach and serve immediately.

Serves 4

Notes
● *Steamed chicory or fresh watercress may be used instead of spinach.*
● *Cubed Blaauwkrantz cheese and coarsely chopped walnuts or pecan nuts may be used instead of feta cheese and pine kernels.*
● *This salad does not keep well.*

Baby marrow and carrot cake

500 ml cake flour
125 ml white sugar
125 ml firmly packed brown sugar
15 ml baking powder
2 ml salt
5 ml ground cinnamon
250 ml chopped walnuts or pecan nuts
250 ml grated baby marrows ($\pm$4 medium-large)
250 ml grated carrots ($\pm$4 medium)
1 egg, well-beaten
75 ml sunflower oil
125 ml milk
sliced oranges, mineolas or persimmons for decoration

Stir together flour, white and brown sugar, baking powder, salt, cinnamon, nuts, baby marrows and carrots. Combine egg, oil and milk until well-blended. Add to carrot and baby marrow mixture and stir until just blended. Pour into a greased and floured 22 cm ring pan and bake in a pre-heated oven at 180°C for 1 hour, or until golden and firm to the touch. Cool in pan for 5 minutes before turning out onto a wire rack to cool completely. Serve sliced with fresh sliced fruit garnish.

Serves 4-6

Note
● *The baby marrow and carrot cake can be made up to 2 days in advance. Decorate just before serving.*

Poolside buffet

(Menu for 6-8)

Smoked salmon and shrimp parcels

Veal sausage and mushroom phyllo twists

Carrot-filled roulade with creamy dill sauce

Chicken mousseline and vegetable terrine
with basil vinaigrette

Asparagus and banana peppers
with spring onion dressing

Red cabbage and feta cheese salad
with pecan nuts

Apricot fool

Iced mint tea

Smoked salmon and shrimp parcels

500 g thinly sliced smoked salmon
60 ml milk or cream
500 g smooth cottage cheese
60 ml finely chopped fresh dill
60 ml finely chopped capers
500 g shrimps, cooked and shelled
salt and freshly ground black pepper

Trim salmon into strips approximately 8 x 14 cm. Purée trimmings with milk or cream and combine with the cottage cheese. Add dill and capers and fold in shrimps. Season to taste with salt and pepper. Place a spoonful of mixture on each salmon strip and roll up into a parcel. Tie securely with chives or fennel stalks. Arrange on a serving dish and serve with toast fingers, lemon twists and extra black pepper.
Serves 8

Note
● *Smoked salmon trout may be used instead of salmon.*

Veal sausage and mushroom phyllo twists

4 sheets phyllo pastry, each 40 x 30 cm
75 ml clarified butter
30 ml fine fresh breadcrumbs

Filling
250 g veal sausage meat, crumbled
1 small onion, minced
1 clove garlic, crushed
15 ml butter
250 g button mushrooms, finely chopped
2 ml ground cumin
2 ml chopped fresh mint
65 ml finely chopped fresh parsley leaves
75 g smooth cottage cheese
salt and freshly ground black pepper

First make filling. Cook sausage meat in a large saucepan, stirring constantly until browned. Transfer to a sieve and drain. Sauté onion and garlic in butter in the saucepan over moderately low heat. Add mushrooms and cook until liquid has evaporated. Add cumin and mint and cook for 2 minutes. Transfer mixture to a bowl and leave to cool slightly. Stir in parsley, cottage cheese and salt and pepper to taste.

Put 1 sheet of phyllo on work surface, wipe lightly with clarified butter and sprinkle with 15 ml breadcrumbs. Lay another sheet of phyllo on top and brush lightly with some of the remaining clarified butter. Cut sheets into quarters to form 16 squares. Spoon a little filling (approximately 5 ml) onto each square, gather corners of pastry over filling and twist gently to seal. Continue to make twists as described above. Bake on a baking sheet in a pre-heated oven at 200°C for 10-12 minutes.
Makes about 32

Veal sausage and mushroom phyllo twists

Carrot-filled roulade with creamy dill sauce

Roulade
45 ml butter
100 ml cake flour
300 ml milk
freshly grated nutmeg
salt and freshly ground pepper
4 large eggs, separated
125 ml freshly grated Parmesan cheese
2 ml cream of tartar
fresh dill sprigs for decoration

Carrot filling
500 g carrots, thinly sliced (±8 medium carrots)
15 ml softened butter
30 ml thick cream
125 g ricotta cheese
30 ml snipped fresh dill
salt and freshly ground black pepper

Creamy dill sauce
200 ml sour cream or natural yoghurt
30 ml snipped fresh dill
salt and freshly ground pepper

Melt butter in a saucepan. Stir in flour and cook, stirring, for 3 minutes. Add milk, stirring constantly, and simmer for 5 minutes more, still stirring. Add nutmeg and salt and pepper to taste. Transfer mixture to a bowl. Whisk in egg yolks carefully, one at a time, so that mixture doesn't curdle. Whisk in Parmesan cheese. Beat egg whites with a pinch of salt until frothy. Add cream of tartar and beat until stiff peaks form. Fold egg whites into mixture, spread batter into a 35 x 25 cm swiss roll pan or flat pan lined with buttered and floured waxproof paper. Bake in a pre-heated oven at 180°C for 25 minutes or until golden and firm to the touch. Remove from oven; leave to cool for 5 minutes. Cover with a sheet of buttered waxproof paper, buttered side down, with a dishtowel over it. Place another baking sheet over towel and turn roulade over. Remove carefully from pan. Remove waxproof paper carefully from underside of roulade.

Make filling while roulade is baking. Steam carrots until tender (5-10 minutes). Drain very well. Purée carrots with butter and cream until well-blended but still coarse. Add ricotta cheese, dill and salt and pepper to taste. Spread filling over warm roulade in an even layer, leaving a 2 cm border all round. Roll roulade up like a swiss roll, using the dish towel as an aid. Transfer to a serving platter and decorate with sprigs of fresh dill just before serving.

To make sauce, combine sour cream or yoghurt, dill and salt and pepper to taste.

Serve sliced, with sauce.
Serves 6-8

Notes
● *The sauce may be omitted, or the sour cream omitted and low-fat natural yoghurt used instead.*
● *The carrot-filled roulade may be made the day before but the dill sauce should be made just before serving.*

Chicken mousseline and vegetable terrine

250 ml puréed watercress
50 g brown mushrooms, thickly sliced
100 g green beans, steamed and cooled
6 artichoke bottoms, steamed, cooled and sliced
100 g young carrots, steamed and cooled (±2 medium carrots)
50 g *mangetouts* or young peas, steamed and cooled
50 g broccoli florets, steamed and cooled (optional)
100 g baby marrows, steamed, cooled and halved lengthwise
   (±4 baby marrows)

Chicken mousseline
200 g uncooked, skinned chicken breasts
1 egg white
200 ml thick cream or sour cream
salt and freshly ground pepper

First make mousseline. Mince chicken very finely and place in a stainless steel bowl held in a larger bowl of crushed ice. Work in egg white with a spatula, then add cream, to make a fine mousse. Season with salt and pepper and refrigerate for 2 hours. Butter a 1 litre terrine or loaf pan and line base with buttered waxproof paper.
   Mix a quarter of the mousseline with watercress purée. Spoon in watercress mixture. Make successive layers of vegetables (one variety to a layer) on top, separating layers with a layer of chicken mousseline. Cover terrine and place in a larger pan of boiling water reaching halfway up sides of terrine. Bake in a pre-heated oven at 150°C for 25-30 minutes, or until firm to the touch. Remove and cool. Refrigerate for at least 8 hours before unmoulding and serving with basil vinaigrette.
Serves 6-8

Notes
● *The chicken mousseline may be prepared in a food processor. Chop the chicken with the steel blade, then add the egg white and cream, and process to make a fine mousse. The watercress may also be puréed in a food processor.*
● *The vegetable terrine can be made up to a day in advance, and stored in the refrigerator.*

Basil vinaigrette

5 ml salt
1 ml freshly ground white pepper
30 ml white wine vinegar
100 ml olive oil
30 ml very finely chopped fresh basil

Mix salt, pepper and vinegar in a small bowl until salt has dissolved. Stir in olive oil and chopped basil. Serve with chicken mousseline and vegetable terrine*.
Makes 150 ml

Note
● *Basil vinaigrette should be made just before serving.*

Chicken mousseline and vegetable terrine

Iced mint tea

Asparagus and banana peppers with spring onion dressing

800 g fresh green asparagus
4 banana peppers, seeded and sliced

Spring onion dressing
50 ml olive oil
3 spring onions, thinly sliced
1 clove garlic, crushed
5 ml crushed coriander seeds
5 ml snipped fresh fennel
100 ml dry white wine
juice of ½ lemon
salt and freshly ground black pepper

Steam asparagus very lightly (about 5 minutes). Drain and allow to cool. Place on a flat serving dish and sprinkle pepper slices over.
   Combine dressing ingredients in a screw-top jar and shake to blend. Toss with asparagus and peppers just before serving.
Serves 8

Notes
● *If fresh asparagus is unavailable, use lightly steamed broccoli florets instead.*
● *If banana peppers are not available, use 1 green pepper, seeded and sliced, instead.*
● *A herbed yoghurt dressing also goes very well with this salad. Combine 250 ml natural yoghurt, 1 clove garlic, crushed, 5 ml each chopped fresh chives, marjoram and savory, salt and freshly ground pepper to taste. Use instead of spring onion dressing.*

Iced mint tea
Brew tea to desired strength and pour into a glass jug. Allow to cool, then chill in refrigerator for 2 hours. Add ice cubes, fresh mint sprigs and thin lemon slices.

Red cabbage and feta cheese salad with pecan nuts

750 g red cabbage, shredded
500 g feta cheese, cubed
200 g pecan nuts

Dressing
juice of 2 small lemons
60 ml sunflower oil
20 ml honey
salt and freshly ground black pepper

Combine dressing ingredients, beating well. Toss shredded cabbage in dressing, cover and set aside for 1 hour. Just before serving, add feta cheese and nuts, and toss salad to combine.
Serves 8

Apricot fool

250 g dried apricots
60 ml sugar
60 ml Van der Hum liqueur
500 ml thick cream
8 almond macaroons

Soak apricots overnight in water to cover. Simmer in a small saucepan with sugar for 5 minutes. Purée mixture and leave to cool completely. Add Van der Hum. Beat cream until stiff and fold into apricot mixture. Spoon into individual glasses or bowls and serve immediately topped with crumbled almond macaroons.
Serves 8

Note
● *Low-fat yoghurt may be used instead of cream. Drain yoghurt through cheesecloth to obtain a firmer texture. Do not beat – simply fold into apricot mixture.*

Puff pastry

250 g butter
250 g cake flour mixed with 2 ml salt
1 egg
±100 ml water
juice of ½ lemon
90 g cake flour
5 ml cream of tartar

Freeze butter, and cool flour and salt mixture in refrigerator. Sift flour, grate half the butter and rub it into flour with your fingertips. Beat egg, water and lemon juice and stir into flour and butter mixture. Work to a stiff dough with your fingertips. Turn dough out onto a board. Sift 90 g flour and cream of tartar, and grate remaining butter. Sift a little flour and cream of tartar mixture onto butter. Roll pastry into a rectangle on a lightly floured surface. Sprinkle grated butter over ⅔ of pastry, and fold remaining third over butter. Sprinkle liberally with flour and cream of tartar mixture. Roll out again, sprinkle with a little flour and cream of tartar mixture and fold in half. Repeat 2-3 times, sprinkling with a little flour and cream of tartar mixture after each rolling. Wrap in foil and place in refrigerator for 1 hour before use.
Makes 500 g

Shortcrust pastry

250 g cake flour
2 ml salt
175 g butter or margarine
75 ml iced water
15 ml fresh lemon juice

Sift flour and salt into a mixing bowl. Cut or rub in butter or margarine until mixture resembles coarse crumbs. Sprinkle water and lemon juice on crumbs and press lightly. Do not knead, or the pastry will be too heavy. Wrap in waxproof paper and chill until needed.
Makes 500 g

Creamy cheese tartlets

200 g shortcrust* or puff pastry*

Filling
30 ml grated Parmesan cheese
10 ml flour
2 eggs, separated
1 egg yolk
100 ml natural yoghurt
15 ml butter, cut into small pieces
freshly grated nutmeg
sugar
salt and freshly ground pepper

Lightly oil a patty pan. Roll dough out thinly and use to line the hollows. To make filling, combine cheese with flour, 3 egg yolks and yoghurt. Pass mixture through a fine sieve into a saucepan and add butter, a pinch each of nutmeg, sugar and pepper and very little salt. Stir over medium heat until butter has melted. Remove from heat. Beat egg whites until stiff and fold into filling. Spoon mixture into patty pan and bake in a pre-heated oven at 180°C for 10-15 minutes, or until filling is set and pastry is golden brown. Serve hot or cold.
Makes 12

Note
● *Make the tartlets a day in advance and pack in airtight plastic containers.*

Rosemary-baked chicken portions

1,5 kg chicken portions
500 ml natural yoghurt
75 ml dry white breadcrumbs
75 ml grated Parmesan cheese
65 ml chopped fresh rosemary (or 45 ml dried rosemary)
5 ml salt
5 ml freshly ground black pepper
2 ml paprika
1 egg, beaten
45 ml sunflower oil

Place chicken portions in a large bowl and pour yoghurt over. Refrigerate for 1 hour. Combine breadcrumbs, cheese, rosemary, salt, pepper and paprika in a dish. Remove chicken portions from yoghurt, dip in beaten egg, then coat in breadcrumb mixture. Place, skin side up, in an oiled baking dish and drizzle with oil. Bake in a pre-heated oven at 180°C for 50 minutes, or until crisp and brown. Drain on absorbent paper. Serve either hot or cold.
Serves 4-6

Note
● *Prepare chicken a day in advance and pack in an airtight plastic container.*

Creamy cheese tartlets (top left), rosemary-baked chicken portions, lettuce and watercress salad with walnut dressing (front)

Smoked haarders

4 fresh haarders, cleaned and gutted
10 ml salt
5 ml chicken stock powder
2 ml freshly ground black pepper
2 ml sugar
15 ml flour

Salt haarders inside and out with 5 ml salt and refrigerate until firm. Combine remaining salt, stock powder, pepper, sugar and flour and rub into fish, inside and out. Sprinkle 15-20 ml untreated oak or other hardwood shavings into a large deep heavy-based saucepan (preferably cast iron) with a tight-fitting lid. Place fish in a metal container slightly smaller than the saucepan and stand it on a trivet over wood shavings. Close outer saucepan tightly with lid. Smoke on stove on high for 12 minutes, then reduce heat to medium and smoke for 12 minutes. Switch stove off, but do not remove saucepan for 15 minutes. Serve hot or cold.
Serves 4

Notes

• Do not remove lid during smoking. If lid doesn't fit tightly, cover saucepan with foil before closing it with the lid.
• Oak shavings may be bought at hardware stores or barbeque shops. Wineries may also stock the shavings. Buy only untreated shavings.
• Smoke haarders a day or two in advance and store in the refrigerator. Pack in an airtight plastic container.

Herb butter
Combine 250 g slightly softened butter with 100 ml finely chopped fresh tarragon, parsley, chives or basil. Form into a roll, wrap in waxproof paper and chill until firm. Pack the herb butter separately and serve on freshly cut chunks of French bread.

Lettuce and watercress salad with walnut dressing

1 large butter lettuce, separated into leaves
300 g watercress, trimmed

Walnut dressing
100 ml sunflower oil
30 ml fresh lemon juice
15 ml white wine vinegar
30 ml ground walnuts
5 ml salt
freshly ground black pepper

Toss lettuce leaves and watercress in a salad bowl. Combine dressing ingredients in a screw-top and shake until well-blended. Pour over salad and toss just before serving.
Serves 4

Note

• Pack the salad and dressing separately and combine just before serving.

Nut-stuffed fresh pears

Cucumber ribbons with tomato salsa

2 large sweetslice cucumbers, halved and seeds removed
15 ml salt

Tomato salsa
500 g large ripe tomatoes, skinned, seeded and chopped
3 spring onions, thinly sliced
1 large clove garlic, crushed
5 ml seeded and minced red pepper (optional)
15 ml white wine vinegar
1 ml sugar
30 ml olive or sunflower oil
salt and freshly ground black pepper

Cut cucumbers lengthwise into thin strips, to make them look like ribbon noodles. Toss in a bowl with salt and set aside for 10 minutes. Combine salsa ingredients in a bowl, seasoning to taste with salt and pepper. Drain cucumbers in a colander, rinse well under cold water and pat dry with absorbent paper. Spread onto a serving platter and mound salsa in centre.
Serves 4-6

Notes

• If American sweetslice cucumbers are not available, English cucumbers may be used instead. Do not peel the cucumbers before use.
• Cucumber ribbons and salsa may be prepared a few hours in advance. Pack in an airtight container.

Nut-stuffed fresh pears

4 ripe dessert pears
fresh lemon juice

Nut stuffing
65 ml chopped hazelnuts
30 ml chopped pine kernels
65 ml chunky cottage cheese
30 ml heated honey

Halve pears lengthwise and core, leaving stems intact. Sprinkle flesh with lemon juice to prevent discolouring. To make stuffing, combine all ingredients until just blended and pile in hollows in pears just before serving.
Serves 4

Notes
● *Halved and seeded papinos may be used instead of pears. Allow 1 half per person.*
● *Halve and core pears, sprinkle with lemon juice and pack in an airtight container. Make stuffing and pack separately.*

Cucumber ribbons with tomato salsa

Chilled white sangria

2 x 750 ml bottles dry white wine
65 ml orange liqueur
30 ml sugar
125 ml halved sultana grapes
5 orange slices, halved
½ Starking apple, cored and thinly sliced

Combine wine, orange liqueur and sugar in a large jug. Stir well. Add fruit and chill, stirring occasionally, for 2 hours. Serve in glasses over ice cubes.
Serves 4

Notes
● *Sangria may be made up to 24 hours in advance and stored, covered, in the refrigerator.*
● *For transporting, pour sangria into a large thermos flask, and pack ice cubes separately.*
● *Instead of dry white wine and orange liqueur, use dry red wine and 65 ml brandy, and use lemon instead of orange slices. The grapes may be omitted.*

Tandoori chicken grill

(Menu for 4)

Tandoori chicken

Coconut rice

Naan bread

Spicy green beans

Cucumber, tomato and banana raita

Litchis and mangoes with pawpaw sauce

Chilled beer

Tandoori chicken with coconut rice

Tandoori chicken

2 x 1 kg chickens
10 ml salt
75-100 ml melted butter or sunflower oil
1 ml crushed saffron threads

Marinade
50 ml fresh lemon juice
10 ml crushed coriander seeds
5 ml crushed cumin seeds
250 ml natural yoghurt
1 onion, sliced
3 cloves garlic, crushed
15 ml peeled and chopped fresh ginger
5 ml ground cinnamon
2 ml ground turmeric or saffron
5 ml dried red pepper flakes or 2 ml Tabasco sauce
2 ml red food colouring

Halve chickens and make slits in the flesh with a sharp knife. Rub chickens with salt and place them in a large flat dish. Combine marinade ingredients and pour over chickens. Marinate for at least 5 hours, but preferably overnight.

Remove chickens from marinade and baste with the melted butter or oil mixed with saffron. Grill under a pre-heated grill for 5 minutes on both sides, then reduce heat and cook until done (15-20 minutes). (The skin should be crisp.) Serve hot with coconut rice*.
Serves 4

Notes
● *Tandoori chicken can also be grilled over hot coals.*
● *The marinade can be thickened with 10 ml cornflour and served as a sauce with the chicken. More yoghurt and Tabasco sauce may be added, to taste. The sauce goes particularly well with boiled couscous.*
● *For slimmers, remove the skins before marinating chicken, and reduce the quantity of butter or oil used for grilling to 25 ml. Serve with boiled rice instead of coconut rice.*

Coconut rice

750 ml boiling water
375 ml desiccated coconut
45 ml butter
1 onion, chopped
375 ml uncooked long grain rice
5 ml salt
5 ml crushed cardamom seeds
toasted shredded coconut for garnish (optional)

Pour boiling water over coconut and leave to soak for 30 minutes. Strain liquid, pressing coconut against the sieve to extract all the juices. Discard coconut. Melt butter in a saucepan, add onion and sauté for 5 minutes, or until golden. Add rice and fry for 5 minutes. Add coconut liquid, salt and cardamom seeds and boil, covered, until done and liquid has been absorbed (about 20 minutes). Fluff rice with a fork and serve garnished with toasted coconut.
Serves 4-6

Naan bread

1 kg bread flour
1 x 10 g packet instant dried yeast
20 ml salt
500 ml warm water

Combine flour, yeast and salt in a bowl. Adding water gradually, mix to a stiff dough. Turn out onto a lightly floured surface and knead well for about 10 minutes: dough should be smooth and elastic. Cover and allow to rise until doubled in bulk (30-45 minutes). Punch dough down and divide into 12 balls. Roll each ball out into a round on a lightly floured surface. Place rounds on greased baking sheets and allow to rise again until doubled in bulk. Bake in a pre-heated oven at 250°C for 5-7 minutes, or until just puffed and very lightly browned.
Makes 12

Notes
● *Mix the dough for the naan bread ahead of time and store in the freezer. To use, thaw and allow to rise, then proceed as described in the recipe.*
● *Leftover bread can be wrapped tightly in plastic and stored in the freezer for up to 1 month.*

Spicy green beans

25 ml sunflower oil
2-3 spring onions, coarsely chopped
1 green pepper, seeded and chopped
2 cloves garlic, crushed
5 ml ground cumin
5 ml mustard seeds (optional)
5 ml curry powder
2 ml ground turmeric
500 g young green beans, lightly cooked
250 ml desiccated coconut

Heat oil in a large frying pan and sauté onions and green pepper until onions are transparent (about 5 minutes). Add garlic and cook for 1 minute more. Add cumin, mustard seeds, curry powder and turmeric and cook for 2 minutes. Add green beans and coconut and stir-fry for 1-2 minutes.
Serves 4

Note
● *Cauliflower may be used instead of green beans. Break a medium cauliflower into small florets, and steam for 5 minutes. Continue as above.*

Cucumber, tomato and banana raita

2 small sweetslice cucumbers, sliced
500 ml buttermilk
2 ripe tomatoes, skinned and chopped
1 small onion, chopped
50 ml chopped fresh mint
1 ml freshly ground black pepper
5 ml salt
2 large bananas, sliced
5 ml fresh lemon juice

Combine cucumbers, buttermilk, tomatoes, onion, mint, pepper and salt in a bowl. Sprinkle bananas with lemon juice and add to vegetables in bowl. Combine and serve immediately.
Serves 4

Notes
• *Make raita with low-fat yoghurt or chunky cottage cheese instead of buttermilk for slimmers.*
• *The raita can be prepared up to 2 hours in advance, adding the banana just before serving.*

From left: Naan bread, spicy green beans, litchis and mangoes with pawpaw sauce, and cucumber, tomato and banana raita

Litchis and mangoes with pawpaw sauce

500 g fresh litchis, peeled and stoned
2 large fibreless mangoes, peeled and sliced

Pawpaw sauce
1 very ripe pawpaw, peeled and seeded
25 ml fresh lemon juice
sugar to taste

Combine litchis and mangoes and spoon into 4 individual serving bowls. Purée pawpaw with lemon juice and sugar and pour over fruit just before serving.
Serves 4

Note
• *Prepare the pawpaw purée a few hours in advance and store, covered, in the refrigerator.*

From left: **Fried calamari,**
kofta kebabs,
spanakopita triangles,
dolmades and falafel

Middle Eastern mezes

(Menu for 8)

Fried calamari

Kofta kebabs

Spanakopita triangles

Dolmades

Falafel

Feta cheese and olives

Brinjal pâté

Tzatziki

Taramasalata

Hummus

Burghul

Anchovy and tomato salad
with vinaigrette dressing

Fresh dates

Salted pistachio nuts

Honeyed coconut cakes

Ouzo   Retzina

Kofta kebabs

500 g lamb or steak mince
5 ml ground coriander seeds
5 ml ground cumin seeds
15 ml chopped fresh mint
15 ml chopped fresh parsley or coriander leaves
salt and freshly ground black pepper

Combine mince with remaining ingredients and form mixture into small balls. Thread onto bamboo skewers and grill, turning often, for 10 minutes.
Serves 8

Notes
● *Mince may also be formed into a 'sausage' around skewers. Mince lamb or steak mince very finely a second time, press firmly around skewers and place in the freezer for 15-20 minutes to harden slightly before grilling.*
● *Chilli powder or Tabasco sauce to taste may be added to mince for spicier kebabs.*
● *Kofta kebabs may be made a few hours in advance and refrigerated until ready to grill.*

Feta cheese and olives
Cube 250 g feta cheese and toss lightly in a bowl with black olives. Drizzle olive oil over and serve.

Fried calamari

250 g calamari
100 ml cake flour
salt and freshly ground black pepper
sunflower oil for deep frying
lemon wedges for garnish

Slice calamari into rings. Mix together flour and seasoning, and toss calamari in seasoned flour just before ready to serve. Deep-fry in oil until crisp (about 5 minutes). Serve hot, garnished with lemon wedges.
Serves 8

Spanakopita triangles

9 sheets phyllo pastry
200 g butter, melted

Filling
500 g spinach, coarse stems removed
1 onion, finely chopped
50 ml butter
250 g feta cheese, crumbled
2 ml dried oregano, crumbled
freshly grated nutmeg
salt and freshly ground black pepper

Stack phyllo pastry between 2 sheets waxproof paper and cover with a dampened dish towel while making filling. Wash spinach well, then cook with no additional water other than the water clinging to leaves, in a large saucepan, covered, over low heat for 3 minutes or until wilted. Squeeze spinach dry, chop finely and transfer to a bowl. Sauté onion in butter in a small frying pan over medium heat, stirring, until transparent (about 5 minutes). Transfer to bowl containing spinach. Add feta cheese, oregano, nutmeg, salt and pepper and mix well. Working quickly to prevent phyllo pastry from drying out, put 1 sheet on a work surface, brush it lightly with melted butter and halve lengthwise. Fold each half in half lengthwise and brush with melted butter. Place 10 ml spinach mixture in a corner of each strip and fold pastry over to enclose filling and form a triangle. Continue to fold strip in triangle shape. Repeat until all the pastry and filling have been used. Place triangles on lightly greased baking sheets, brush with melted butter and bake in a pre-heated oven at 190°C for 20 minutes, or until puffed and golden. Serve hot.

Makes 18

Note
● *Spanakopita may also be baked as 1 large pie. Using 8 sheets phyllo pastry, brush 4 of them as described above and use to line a large ovenproof dish. Add filling and top with remaining 4 sheets phyllo pastry, brushed with melted butter. Bake in a pre-heated oven at 190°C for 25 minutes or until puffed and golden.*

Dolmades

24 large canned vine leaves in brine, drained, or fresh
　　vine leaves
250 ml natural yoghurt

Filling
125 ml uncooked long grain rice
15 ml chopped fresh mint
15 ml chopped fresh parsley
45 ml olive or sunflower oil
250 g brown mushrooms, finely chopped
2 cloves garlic, crushed
60 g black olives, stoned and chopped
salt and freshly ground black pepper

Blanch fresh vine leaves in boiling water for 3 minutes. Drain. To make filling, cook rice in boiling salted water until just tender (about 20 minutes). Drain and return to saucepan. Stir in herbs, oil, mushrooms, garlic and olives. Cook over medium heat, covered, for 10 minutes, or until mushrooms are soft and flavours well-blended. Season with salt and pepper to taste. To fill each vine leaf, lay it flat and place 15 ml stuffing in centre. Roll up from stalk end, tucking in edges as you go. Pack parcels in a large saucepan, pour in just enough water to cover and cook over medium heat for 35-40 minutes. Drain and serve, hot or cold, with natural yoghurt.

Makes 24

Note
● *Dolmades may be prepared up to a day in advance and chilled until needed.*

Falafel

450 g cooked chickpeas
1 egg, lightly beaten
2 ml turmeric
30 ml chopped fresh coriander leaves or parsley
1 ml ground cumin seeds
1 ml cayenne pepper
1 clove garlic, crushed
15 ml tahini (sesame paste)
100 ml cracked wheat, soaked and dried
salt and freshly ground black pepper
100 ml cake flour
sunflower oil for deep-frying

Combine chickpeas, egg, turmeric, coriander or parsley, cumin, cayenne pepper, garlic, tahini and cracked wheat in a blender or food processor. Blend until smooth then season with salt and pepper. Shape mixture into 2 cm diameter balls and flatten them slightly. Dust with flour and deep-fry in hot oil until lightly browned (about 5 minutes). Drain well on absorbent paper and serve hot.

Serves 8

Note
● *Tahini is available from health stores and some supermarkets.*

Brinjal pâté

1 large brinjal
sunflower oil
1 slice white bread, crust removed
1 clove garlic, crushed
1 spring onion, finely chopped
15 ml finely chopped fresh parsley
5 ml chopped fresh marjoram
salt and freshly ground black pepper
60 ml olive oil
fresh lemon juice

Brush skin of brinjal with sunflower oil and bake in a pre-
heated oven at 190°C for 40-60 minutes, or until soft. Set aside
to cool. Halve brinjal and scoop flesh into a blender or food
processor. Soak bread in cold water and press dry. Add to brinjal with garlic, spring onion, herbs, salt and pepper. Blend until
smooth. Gradually add oil, beating constantly. Adjust seasoning if necessary, and add lemon juice to taste. Serve with vegetable crudités or toast fingers.
Makes about 250 ml

Note
● *Brinjal pâté may be made up to a day in advance and chilled until
needed.*

Tzatziki

1 English cucumber, peeled and finely diced
salt and freshly ground black pepper
2 cloves garlic, crushed
30 ml finely chopped fresh mint
250 ml natural yoghurt
15 ml fresh lemon juice
45 ml thick cream (optional)
chopped fresh mint for decoration

Place cucumber in a sieve, sprinkle with salt and leave to drain
for 1 hour. Mix remaining ingredients (except fresh mint) and
season to taste. Rinse cucumber in cold water and combine
with yoghurt mixture. Serve decorated with chopped mint.
Makes about 500 ml

Taramasalata

1 slice white bread, crust removed
1 clove garlic, crushed
250 g smoked fish roe, skinned
150 ml sunflower oil
150 ml olive oil
lemon juice
freshly ground black pepper

Soak bread in cold water and press dry. Place in a bowl with garlic and fish roe. Beat in oils drop by drop, using a wooden spoon
or electric hand mixer, or blend in a blender or food processor.
Season to taste with lemon juice and black pepper.
Makes about 500 ml

Note
● *Taramasalata may be prepared a few hours in advance and
refrigerated.*

Hummus

450 g cooked chickpeas
100 ml cold water
2 cloves garlic, crushed
150 ml tahini
juice of 1 lemon
7 ml salt
freshly ground black pepper
pinch ground cumin
pinch chilli powder
chopped fresh coriander leaves for decoration

Blend chickpeas and water in a blender or food processor.
Gradually beat in garlic, tahini and lemon juice to taste. The
mixture should spread easily – add a little more water if it is
very thick. Season with salt and pepper, cumin and chilli
powder and decorate with coriander leaves.
Makes about 500 ml

Note
● *Hummus may be prepared a few hours in advance and
refrigerated.*

Burghul

75 g cracked wheat
4 tomatoes, skinned, seeded and finely chopped
½ English cucumber, finely chopped
1 green pepper, seeded and finely chopped
½ medium onion, finely chopped
60 ml chopped fresh parsley
15 ml finely chopped fresh mint
juice of 2 lemons
60 ml olive oil
salt and freshly ground black pepper

Soak cracked wheat in cold water to cover for 1 hour. Drain well, wrap in a clean dish towel and press out all excess moisture. Spread wheat out on a tray to dry. Place prepared vegetables in a mixing bowl with wheat. Stir in parsley, mint, lemon juice and olive oil, season well with salt and pepper and serve.
Serves 8

Note
● *Burghul may be prepared up to 3 hours in advance and stored in the refrigerator until needed.*

Anchovy and tomato salad with vinaigrette dressing

50 g canned anchovy fillets in oil
100 ml milk
2 ripe tomatoes, skinned, seeded and coarsely chopped
3 hard-boiled eggs, cut into wedges

Vinaigrette dressing
45 ml olive or sunflower oil
20 ml fresh lemon juice or white vinegar
salt and pepper

Drain oil from anchovies and soak them in milk for 1 hour. Drain, pat dry with a paper towel, and chop coarsely.
To make vinaigrette dressing, combine ingredients in a screw-top jar and shake well to blend.
Toss salad and dressing, and serve.
Serves 8

From left: Hummus, brinjal pâté, tzatziki, taramasalata, burghul, anchovy and tomato salad with vinaigrette dressing

Salted pistachio nuts
Pistachio nuts are available in their shells or shelled. To salt them, toss the shelled nuts in coarse salt and store them in an airtight container until needed. You will need about 200 g for 8 people.

Honeyed coconut cakes

500 ml cake flour
250 ml sugar
10 ml baking powder
125 ml desiccated coconut
2 large eggs, lightly beaten
150 g butter, melted and cooled
250 ml natural yoghurt
2 ml coconut essence
75 ml honey
25 ml butter

Sift flour, sugar and baking powder into a mixing bowl and stir in coconut. In another bowl, stir eggs, butter, yoghurt and coconut essence and blend well. Stir into flour mixture until just combined. (Mixture should be lumpy.) Pour batter into a greased deep patty pan or muffin pan and bake in a pre-heated oven at 190°C for 10-15 minutes, or until a skewer inserted in centre comes out clean.
Melt together honey and 25 ml butter, and pour over coconut cakes while they're still hot.
Makes 12

Note
● *Bake honeyed coconut cakes up to 2 days beforehand and store in airtight containers until needed.*

Mexican braai

(Menu for 4)

Braaied prawns with peri-peri sauce

Tacos

Mexican salad with coriander dressing

Chilli pot

Avocado ice cream

Tequila

Tacos filled with Mexican salad with coriander dressing: braaied prawns with peri-peri sauce

Braaied prawns with peri-peri sauce

24 large prawns or 12 langoustines

Peri-peri sauce
200 ml sunflower oil
200 g butter
2 ml Tabasco sauce or ground peri-peri
1 clove garlic, crushed

First make sauce. Heat oil and butter in a saucepan, stir in Tabasco sauce or peri-peri and garlic. Brush prawns with peri-peri sauce and grill over hot coals for 5-7 minutes (10-15 minutes for langoustines), turning and basting often with sauce.
Serves 4

Note
● *For slimmers, use a little butter and lemon juice instead of peri-peri sauce to baste the prawns or langoustines.*

Tacos

300 g bread flour
60 g coarse yellow mealie meal
100 g cornflour
5 ml salt
10 ml baking powder
100 g margarine
250 ml water

Combine dry ingredients. Cut in margarine and rub until mixture resembles coarse crumbs. Add water and mix to a soft dough. Knead until smooth and elastic on a lightly floured surface. Shape dough into 12 balls, cover and leave for 15 minutes. Roll each ball out to a 15 mm diameter circle on a lightly floured surface. Heat an ungreased heavy-based frying pan or griddle and cook tacos on both sides until lightly browned. Fold immediately into a U-shape over a wooden spoon handle and allow to dry. Serve stuffed with Mexican salad*, or with salad ingredients of your choice.
Makes 12

Note
● *Taco shells may be made up to a month in advance and stored in an airtight container or frozen. To use, heat briefly in a hot oven to crisp before filling.*

Mexican salad with coriander dressing

1 onion, chopped
1 small lettuce, thinly shredded
2 ripe tomatoes, skinned and chopped
250 ml lightly cooked or canned whole corn kernels
½ green pepper, seeded and chopped
1 ripe avocado pear, sliced
4 rashers bacon, crisply fried

Coriander dressing
50 ml vinegar
5 ml salt
100 ml olive oil
5 ml crushed coriander seeds

Layer onion, lettuce, tomatoes, corn kernels and green pepper in a glass bowl. Arrange avocado pear slices on top. Crumble bacon over. Combine dressing ingredients, shake well in a screw-top jar until well-blended and pour over salad just before serving. Serve with taco shells, so that the salad can be placed inside for eating.
Serves 4-6

Chilli pot

250 ml finely chopped onion (±2 onions)
3 large cloves garlic, crushed
15 ml sunflower oil
250 g cooked kidney beans or sugar beans
800 g canned tomato purée
5 ml chilli powder
10 ml dried oregano
2 ml cumin seeds
10 ml salt
10 ripe olives, pitted (optional)

Sauté onion and garlic in heated oil in a cast iron pot until onion is transparent. Add beans, tomato purée, chilli powder, oregano, cumin seeds and salt and cook over medium coals until tender and sauce is well-blended (about 1 hour). Add olives just before serving.
Serves 4-6

Note
● *Cook the beans for the chilli pot the night before. Soak in water to cover for at least 6 hours, then cook in the same water until barely tender (45-60 minutes).*

Avocado ice cream

2 large very ripe avocado pears
5 ml fresh lemon juice
15 ml honey or sugar
20 ml tequila
500 ml vanilla ice cream, slightly softened

Peel and stone avocado pear. Purée to a smooth consistency with lemon juice, honey or sugar, and tequila. Combine avocado purée well with vanilla ice cream and spoon into individual sugar-and-salt-frosted glass dishes. Freeze until firm.
Serves 4

Notes
● *To frost dishes, dip rims in lightly beaten egg white, then in a mixture of sugar and coarse salt.*
● *For slimmers, serve **frozen avocado yoghurt** instead of avocado ice cream. Follow the recipe for avocado ice cream, but omit the tequila and use 500 ml low-fat natural yoghurt instead of vanilla ice cream.*

LIGHT LUNCHES

*S*omething light, accompanied by a salad or two, makes the perfect lunch no matter what the time of year. For cooler days, try the quick and easy-to-prepare **Stir-fry special** menu or the **Quiche and soufflé lunch** menu with its delightful variations on the old favourites. If you prefer a salad lunch, there are four **Salad spread** menus to choose from – each of them featuring deliciously different recipes. Savour to the full the dishes on the **Seafood lunch** menu – they're light enough to enjoy and feel satisfied but won't make you too full.

Fish and spinach stir-fry with spring onions

500 g white fish fillets
30 ml olive or sunflower oil
1 clove garlic, crushed
10 ml chopped fresh tarragon or 5 ml dried
5 spring onions, thinly sliced
500 g young spinach leaves, coarsely shredded
65 ml sprinkle nuts
50 ml dry white vermouth
salt and freshly ground pepper

Cut fish fillets into thin strips. Heat oil in a wok or large heavy-based frying pan and stir-fry garlic, tarragon and spring onions for 1 minute. Add fish and stir-fry until opaque (about 3 minutes). Add spinach and sprinkle nuts, and stir-fry for 1 minute. Add Cinzano and cook, covered, for 1 minute. Season, if necessary, and serve hot with fried noodles*.
Serves 4

Fried noodles

125 g spaghettini noodles
sunflower oil for deep-frying

Soak noodles in hot water for 1 minute, then drain well. Transfer to paper towels and pat dry. Pour 5 cm deep oil in a saucepan or deep-frier and heat until very hot. Fry noodles, a handful at a time, in hot oil for 1 minute or until golden. Remove with a slotted spoon and transfer to absorbent paper towels to drain off excess oil. Serve hot.
Serves 4

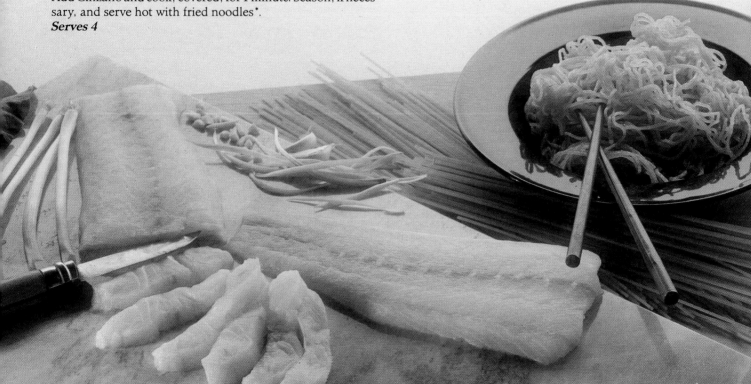

Chinese sweet and sour vegetables

350 ml mangetouts, sugar snap peas or young peas in pods
200 g carrots, cut into julienne strips (±6 medium carrots)
200 g Chinese cabbage, shredded (±1 small cabbage)
300 g oyster mushrooms
125 ml bean sprouts
125 ml sliced water chestnuts
15 ml soy sauce
15 ml sherry
10 ml ginger syrup
1 clove garlic, crushed
30 ml lemon juice
30 ml sunflower oil

Combine all vegetables. Combine remaining ingredients and add with the vegetables to a heated wok or heavy-based frying pan. Toss for 5 minutes. Serve immediately.
Serves 4

Notes
● *Cos lettuce, chicory or spinach may be used if Chinese cabbage is not available.*
● *Salted cashew nuts, finely chopped, make a tasty addition.*
● *If oyster mushrooms are unavailable use slivered button mushrooms instead.*
● *Finely diced preserved ginger may also be added.*

From left: **Ingredients for fish and spinach stir-fry with spring onions, fried noodles, ingredients for amandine of apples and berry fruits, Chinese sweet and sour vegetables**

Amandine of apples and berry fruits

85 g butter
100 ml castor sugar
15 ml fresh lemon juice
3 eggs, separated
50 ml cake flour
100 ml ground almonds
100 ml cornflour
2 Granny Smith apples, peeled and cored
300 g mixed fresh berries (stoned mulberries, loganberries, raspberries, blueberries, strawberries) and/or cherries

Cream butter and castor sugar with lemon juice until light and fluffy. Beat in egg yolks, one at a time, beating well after each addition. Fold in flour, almonds and cornflour. Whisk egg whites until soft peaks form and fold into batter. Slice apples thinly and place in base of 4 greased individual ovenproof dishes. Divide mixed berries between dishes and spread batter over. Bake in pre-heated oven at 200°C for 20 minutes and serve warm or cold.
Serves 4

Notes
● *If fresh berries are unavailable, use drained canned ones.*
● *For a more slimming dessert, beat 3 egg whites with 20 ml sugar and spread over fresh fruit in dishes. Bake in a pre-heated oven at 200°C for 5 minutes to brown and serve immediately.*

First make pastry. Combine butter, cheese and flour and press into a 20 cm ovenproof dish.

To make filling, melt butter over low heat, add flour and stir to make a roux. Add milk and boil until thick, stirring constantly. Remove from stove. Add asparagus and cheese. Beat egg yolks lightly and add to mixture. Beat egg whites until stiff and fold into mixture. Pour into pie crust and bake in a pre-heated oven at 160°C for 30 minutes, or until filling is set. Serve warm or cold.
Serves 4

Notes
● *Canned asparagus tips, drained, may be used if fresh asparagus is unavailable.*
● *To cook fresh asparagus, trim stems and tie spears in bundles of 8-12. Tie the bundles in two places, and stand them upright in a deep saucepan of boiling water with the tips above water level. Cover partially, and cook for 15-20 minutes or until tender. Drain well before use.*
● *For a delicious filling variation, sauté 3 large leeks, trimmed and chopped, in 60 ml butter. Beat 4 eggs with 250 ml cream, add 125 ml grated Cheddar cheese and combine with leeks. Pour into the crust and bake at 160°C for 45-50 minutes or until set. Serve warm or cold.*

Baby marrow soufflé

30 ml butter or margarine
30 ml cake flour
375 ml warm milk
250 ml grated Cheddar cheese
2 ml salt
1 ml pepper
4 eggs, separated
250 ml thinly sliced baby marrows (±4 medium)

Melt butter or margarine over low heat, add flour and stir to make a smooth paste (roux). Add milk and boil, stirring, over medium heat until thickened. Remove from stove and cool slightly. Add cheese, salt, pepper and egg yolks, stirring constantly. Fold in baby marrows. Beat egg whites until stiff and fold into baby marrow mixture. Spoon into a 1 litre soufflé dish and bake in a pre-heated oven at 160°C for 45 minutes, or until risen and golden. Serve immediately.
Serves 4

Fluffy asparagus quiche

Pastry
125 ml grated cold butter
125 ml grated Cheddar cheese
125 ml cake flour

Filling
15 ml butter
30 ml cake flour
250 ml milk
250 ml cooked and chopped fresh green asparagus
125 ml grated Cheddar cheese
2 eggs, separated

Tomato and anchovy quiche with fresh basil

Pastry
500 ml cake flour
250 g smooth cottage cheese
250 g cold butter, grated

Filling
175 g mozzarella cheese, grated
2 eggs, lightly beaten
30 ml cake flour
300 ml milk
salt and freshly ground pepper
250 g ripe tomatoes, skinned and sliced
butter
8 anchovy fillets
10 ml chopped fresh basil

First make the pastry. Combine flour and cottage cheese in a bowl. Add butter and knead to form a smooth dough. Refrigerate for 30 minutes, then roll out on a lightly floured surface and use to line a 20 cm quiche pan.

To make the filling, combine cheese, eggs, flour and sufficient milk to make a soft paste. Spread over pastry dough and season with salt and pepper. Place tomatoes over cheese mixture, dot with butter and season lightly. Bake in pre-heated oven at 180°C for 20-30 minutes, or until filling is set.

Garnish with anchovies and sprinkle with basil. Serve hot or cold.
Serves 4

Note
● *Grated Cheddar cheese may be used instead of mozzarella cheese.*

Carrot salad with lemon and cumin

6 large carrots, cut in julienne strips
grated rind and juice of 1 large lemon
20 ml vodka (optional)
5 ml cumin seeds
freshly ground black pepper

Place carrot julienne strips in a bowl. Combine lemon rind and juice, vodka and cumin seeds in a screw-top jar and shake to blend well. Drizzle over carrots and chill for 15 minutes. Sprinkle with pepper just before serving.
Serves 4

Carrot salad with lemon and cumin

Green salad with avocado vinaigrette

6 chicory leaves
6 Swiss chard leaves
1 small oak lettuce, separated into leaves
1 small 'Baby Gem' lettuce, separated into leaves
6 butter lettuce leaves

Avocado vinaigrette
1/2 small ripe avocado pear
10 ml fresh lemon juice
65 ml sunflower oil
30 ml white wine vinegar
1 clove garlic, crushed
salt and freshly ground black pepper

Tear chicory, chard and lettuce leaves into bite-sized pieces and place in a salad bowl. To make dressing, purée avocado flesh with lemon juice in a food processor or blender. Add remaining ingredients, seasoning to taste with salt and pepper, and blend until smooth. Just before serving, add dressing to greens in salad bowl and toss lightly.
Serves 4

Notes
• *Vary the greens in this salad according to the season and what is available: young spinach leaves or Chinese cabbage leaves, for example, or unusual but handy greens like beet tops, dandelions or nasturtiums.*
• *If avocado pear is not available, use 125 ml lightly cooked and puréed petit pois.*
• *Prepare the avocado vinaigrette a few hours in advance and store in the refrigerator until needed.*

Grapefruit snow

15 ml gelatine
65 ml cold water
250 ml hot water
250 ml sugar
75 ml grapefruit juice (±1 large grapefruit)
grated rind of 1/2 lemon
2 egg whites, stiffly beaten
segments of 1/2 rosé grapefruit for decoration

Soak gelatine in cold water for about 5 minutes, then dissolve in hot water. Stir in sugar, grapefruit juice and lemon rind and strain into a bowl through a fine sieve. Chill in refrigerator until beginning to set, then beat with a whisk until light and foamy. Fold in egg whites and pour into a 1 litre decorative mould rinsed with cold water or sprayed with non-stick cooking spray. Refrigerate until set. Serve decorated with rosé grapefruit segments, from which the membrane has been removed.
Serves 4

Note
• *The grapefruit snow may be prepared the day before and refrigerated until needed. Decorate just before serving.*

Salad spreads

(for 4)

Menu 1

Cucumber mousse with crudités

Calamari noodle salad with pesto

Melon with pecan nuts

Pink soda

Menu 2

Chilled petit pois soup with curried croûtons

Broccoli, avocado and sweet pepper salad

Crayfish-stuffed tomatoes

Lemon granite

White wine spritzer

Menu 3

Herbed ricotta timbales

Fennel and seafood salad

Grapes in jellied hanepoot

Chilled dessert wine

Menu 4

Pistachio, leek and spinach mould

Rare roast beef with black peppercorn dressing

Curried avocado citrus salad

Ginger-poached rhubarb

Lightly chilled Tinta Barocca

Cucumber mousse with crudités

150 g smooth cottage cheese
125 ml thick cream
15 ml gelatine
125 ml chicken stock
1 medium English cucumber
10 ml lemon juice
salt and freshly ground black pepper
fresh vegetables for crudités

Combine cottage cheese and cream until well-blended. Sprinkle gelatine onto cold chicken stock, then heat gently over simmering water until gelatine has dissolved (about 5 minutes). Grate unpeeled cucumber coarsely and drain in a sieve for about 10 minutes. Mix into cottage cheese mixture. Add lemon juice and gelatine, season with salt and pepper and mix well.

Pour into a 1,5 litre mould rinsed with cold water or sprayed with non-stick cooking spray and chill until set. Unmould carefully and serve with vegetable crudités.

For vegetable crudités, trim, wash and slice a selection of fresh vegetables – baby marrows, carrots, green pepper, celery, cucumber, mushrooms, cherry tomatoes – and arrange attractively on a large serving platter.
Serves 4-6

Notes
● *For slimmers, use low fat yoghurt in the mousse instead of cream. First drain yoghurt through cheesecloth for a thicker consistency.*
● *The cucumber mousse can be prepared the day before.*

Calamari noodle salad with pesto

200 g fettuccini
5 ml salt
250 g calamari, cut into rings

Pesto
50 ml chopped fresh basil
30 ml pine kernels
30 ml finely grated Parmesan cheese
20 ml olive oil

Cook fettuccini in boiling salted water until just cooked (about 10 minutes). Drain well, rinse with cold water and place in a strainer to drain completely. Cook calamari in a little water until opaque (about 5-10 minutes). To make pesto, place basil, pine kernels and cheese in a blender. Slowly pour in olive oil while machine is running and blend until smooth and thick. Add calamari to fettuccini, toss with pesto and serve.
Serves 4

Note
● *The calamari and noodle salad and pesto may be prepared separately, up to 5 hours in advance, and chilled until needed. Allow to stand at room temperature for 30 minutes, then combine.*

Melon with pecan nuts

375 ml ripe watermelon balls ($\pm\frac{1}{2}$ small round watermelon)
375 ml ripe spanspek balls (±1 small spanspek)
375 ml ripe Ogen melon balls (±1 small Ogen melon)
125 ml chopped pecan nuts
6 pieces preserved ginger, finely chopped
30 ml honey or ginger syrup
65 ml orange liqueur

Combine watermelon, spanspek and Ogen melon balls in a serving dish and sprinkle with nuts and preserved ginger. Heat honey or ginger syrup to make it liquid, then combine with liqueur and pour over melon. Chill for 30 minutes.
Serves 4

Note
● *For slimmers, serve the dessert without ginger and honey. Sprinkle 5 ml liqueur over each portion just before serving.*

Cucumber mousse with crudités

Chilled petit pois soup with curried croûtons

Chilled petit pois soup with curried croûtons

250 g frozen petit pois
30 ml medium cream sherry
125 ml thick cream
250 ml cold vegetable or chicken stock
50 ml natural yoghurt
2 ml onion juice (optional)
freshly ground black pepper
fresh mint sprigs for garnish

Curried croûtons
75 ml melted butter or margarine
5 ml curry powder
1 clove garlic, crushed, or 1 ml garlic powder
3 thick slices stale bread, crusts removed

Thaw peas slightly, then place in a blender or food processor with sherry and blend. Add cream, stock, yoghurt, onion juice and black pepper and mix lightly. Transfer to a glass bowl and chill for 30 minutes.

To make croûtons, combine butter or margarine with curry and garlic in a large frying pan. Cube bread and stir-fry in curry mixture over medium heat until crisp on all sides.

To serve, place bowl of soup in a larger bowl of crushed ice, garnish with mint and serve hot curried croûtons separately.
Serves 4

Broccoli, avocado and sweet pepper salad

350 g broccoli, trimmed
1 small red sweet pepper, seeded and sliced into rings
1 large avocado pear, peeled and stoned
fresh lemon juice

Garlic vinaigrette
100 ml olive or sunflower oil
30 ml lemon juice
5 ml salt
freshly ground black pepper
1 clove garlic, crushed

Steam broccoli for 4-5 minutes, or until bright green but still crunchy. Refresh under cold running water, drain and place in a bowl with pepper rings. Cut avocado pear into chunks and sprinkle with lemon juice. Combine with broccoli and pepper slices.

To make garlic vinaigrette, combine all ingredients in a screw-top jar and shake until well-blended. Toss with salad ingredients just before serving.
Serves 4-6

Note
• *The dressing for the broccoli, avocado and sweet pepper salad may be prepared a day in advance and refrigerated until needed.*

Crayfish-stuffed tomatoes

4 large ripe tomatoes
10 ml capers for garnish
10 ml chopped fresh parsley for garnish

Stuffing
500 ml cooked crayfish, chopped
1 stalk celery, chopped
1 clove garlic, crushed
150 ml mayonnaise
15 ml tomato paste
15 ml Pernod (optional)
salt and freshly ground pepper

Slice tops off tomatoes and scoop out pulp. Turn tomato shells upside down on absorbent paper and place in refrigerator to drain and chill.

Combine stuffing ingredients. Fill tomatoes with stuffing and serve immediately, garnished with capers and parsley.
Serves 4

Broccoli, avocado and sweet pepper salad

Lemon granite

250 ml fresh lemon juice
20 ml freshly grated lemon rind
375 ml sugar
125 ml dry white wine
375 ml cold water
egg white of 1 large egg

Beat the egg white until frothy.

Combine all ingredients in a large bowl and stir until sugar has dissolved. Transfer to freezer container and freeze until slushy. Beat well to remove ice crystals, return to container and freeze until firm.

Serve scoops heaped in glass bowls.
Serves 4-6

Notes
• *Limes, if available, make a tangy substitute for lemons. Tart oranges could also be used, or grapefruit.*
• *Serve with wafers or paper-thin ginger biscuits.*

Cream cheese and mix in remaining ingredients, seasoning to taste with salt and pepper. Pack into 4 individual moulds and refrigerate, covered, until needed. Turn timbales out and serve.
Serves 4

Note
● *Ricotta timbales may be prepared a day in advance and refrigerated until needed.*

Fennel and seafood salad

250 g shelled prawns
250 g mussels
12 chicory leaves
2 large fennel bulbs, trimmed
8 black olives
fennel sprigs for decoration

Herb marinade
45 ml fresh lemon juice
100 ml olive or sunflower oil
5 ml chopped fresh rosemary
1 clove garlic, crushed
30 ml snipped fresh chives
salt and freshly ground black pepper
15 ml chopped fresh oregano

Steam prawns and mussels for 8-10 minutes, or until the latter open. Combine prawns and mussels in a shallow dish, leaving some mussels in their shells. Combine marinade ingredients and pour over seafood. Marinate in the refrigerator for at least 1 hour, turning seafood occasionally. Arrange chicory leaves around rim of a round serving dish. Chop fennel finely and combine with marinated seafood and olives. Pile all, including marinade, in centre of serving dish. Decorate with fennel sprigs and serve.
Serves 4-6

Notes
● *Canned mussels or prawns can be used instead of fresh ones.*
● *Prepare marinade, and marinate seafood for up to 3 hours in the refrigerator.*

Grapes in jellied hanepoot

1 x 750 ml bottle sweet dessert wine
30 ml gelatine
500 g sultana or other seedless grapes
4-6 sponge fingers

Sprinkle gelatine on 100 ml cold water and allow to dissolve. Heat a quarter of the wine in a saucepan and dissolve gelatine in it, stirring. Then place in a wide bowl with remaining chilled wine and chill in refrigerator. Divide washed and well-dried grapes among 4-6 glass bowls or wine glasses and pour wine jelly over. Chill until set. Serve with sponge fingers.
Serves 4-6

Note
● *For slimmers, use low-alcohol white wine instead of hanepoot.*

Grapes in jellied hanepoot

Herbed ricotta timbales

250 g ricotta cheese
30 ml olive or sunflower oil
30 ml chopped fresh parsley
15 ml snipped fresh chives
15 ml chopped fresh basil
5 ml dried oregano
1 clove garlic, crushed
6-8 ripe olives, pitted and chopped
salt and freshly ground black pepper

Pistachio, leek and spinach mould

50 ml butter
1 kg leeks, washed, trimmed and thinly sliced
4 eggs
250 ml cream or natural yoghurt
30 ml shelled pistachio nuts
salt and freshly ground black pepper
500 g spinach, trimmed and ribs removed
sliced radishes, spring onions and pistachio nuts for garnish

Melt butter in a saucepan and cook leeks, covered, over low heat for 6-8 minutes, or until just tender. Remove from stove and leave to cool. Place in a blender or food processor with eggs and cream or yoghurt and blend to a smooth purée. Stir in most of the pistachio nuts (retaining a few for decoration) and season to taste with salt and pepper. Steam spinach until wilted (about 5 minutes). Butter a 1,5 litre mould and line base and sides with spinach leaves, leaving enough overlapping to enclose filling. Pour leek purée into mould, fold down spinach leaves and cover with buttered waxproof paper. Place mould in a baking pan and pour in sufficient boiling water to come halfway up sides of mould. Bake in a pre-heated oven at 220°C for 30-40 minutes. Remove from oven and leave for 10 minutes before unmoulding onto a serving dish. Surround mould with sliced radishes, spring onions and additional pistachio nuts. Serve hot or cold.
Serves 4-6

Rare roast beef with black peppercorn dressing

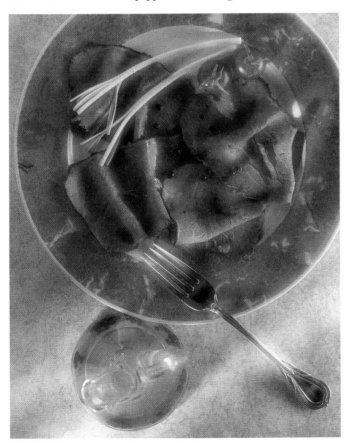

Rare roast beef with black peppercorn dressing

500 g cooked rare roast beef, thinly sliced
4 spring onions, trimmed, for garnish

Black peppercorn dressing
20 ml sunflower oil
15 ml tarragon vinegar
15 ml black peppercorns
1 ml Tabasco sauce
pinch salt

Arrange sliced beef on a serving dish and garnish with spring onion. Combine dressing ingredients in a screw-top jar, shake well to blend and serve separately.
Serves 4

Note
● *Roast 500 g beef in a pre-heated oven at 180°C for 20-25 minutes. The beef can be roasted a day in advance and refrigerated.*

Curried avocado citrus salad

1 grapefruit, segmented and membranes removed
2 mineolas, segmented, or 4 naartjies, segmented and
    membranes removed
1 large avocado pear, peeled and stoned

Curry dressing
15 ml natural yoghurt
15 ml fruit chutney
5 ml curry powder

Halve citrus segments and chop avocado pear into chunks. Combine in a salad bowl. Combine dressing ingredients in a screw-top jar and shake to mix well. Pour over salad and toss just before serving.
Serves 4-6

Ginger-poached rhubarb

750 g rhubarb, peeled and coarsely chopped
30 ml sugar
10 ml ground ginger
300 ml unsweetened orange juice
6 pieces preserved ginger in syrup, chopped

Place rhubarb in a saucepan with sugar and ground ginger, pour over orange juice and poach, covered, until rhubarb is just tender but not mushy (2-3 minutes). Pour into a serving dish, sprinkle with preserved ginger and chill until ready to serve.
Serves 4-6

Notes
● *Take great care not to cook the rhubarb too long, as it becomes mushy very quickly.*
● *Ginger-poached rhubarb may be prepared up to 2 hours in advance.*

Seafood lunch

(Menu for 4)

Potted monkfish with cashews

Mussel, pea and shrimp risotto

Steamed young vegetables
with garlic butter slices

Orange custard

Chilled Chardonnay

Potted monkfish with cashews

Potted monkfish with cashews

400 g monkfish fillets, diced
salt
1 bay leaf
10 ml black peppercorns
200 g butter
fresh lemon juice
2 ml grated nutmeg
salt and freshly ground black pepper
young spinach leaves
75 ml salted cashew nuts, coarsely chopped
cayenne pepper
lemon slices for garnish

Poach diced monkfish fillets in lightly salted water with bay leaf and peppercorns until opaque (about 10 minutes). Drain well. Heat butter and a squeeze of lemon juice in a saucepan over very low heat, add fish and stir for 2-3 minutes. Do not allow to brown. Add nutmeg, salt and pepper. Press mixture into 4 large oiled ramekins and cool. Cover and refrigerate overnight. Arrange spinach leaves on 4 plates and unmould potted monkfish carefully onto them. Sprinkle with nuts and cayenne pepper and serve, garnished with lemon slices.
Serves 4

Note
● *Prepare potted monkfish with cashews the night before and refrigerate until needed.*

Mussel, pea and shrimp risotto

500 g mussels, scrubbed and debearded
45 ml butter
1 medium onion, chopped
1 clove garlic, crushed
250 ml uncooked rice
750 ml hot fish or chicken stock
1 x 110 g can smoked mussels, drained
250 ml (100 g) cooked and shelled shrimps
1/2 green pepper, seeded and sliced
125 ml fresh or frozen young peas
30 ml chopped fresh parsley
10 ml grated lemon rind
freshly ground black pepper

Steam fresh mussels for 5 minutes in water to cover. Drain. Set aside 6 mussels in shells for garnish, and remove remainder from shells. Melt 30 ml butter in a saucepan, add onion and garlic and sauté until onion is transparent (about 5 minutes). Add rice to onion mixture and fry for 2 minutes. Add fish stock and cook over medium heat until liquid is almost absorbed. Add remaining ingredients and heat through. Risotto should be creamy, but not mushy. Season with freshly ground black pepper and serve garnished with unshelled steamed mussels.
Serves 4

Note
● *To save time, leftover cooked rice may be used. Sauté onions and garlic in butter, add rice and remaining ingredients (omitting stock) and toss lightly until heated through.*

Steamed young vegetables with garlic butter slices

150 g young green beans
150 g young carrots (±3-4 carrots)
300 g broccoli florets

Garlic butter slices
75 g butter, softened
2 cloves garlic, crushed
2 ml salt
2 ml finely chopped fresh chives

First make garlic butter slices. Combine ingredients, form into a long narrow roll, wrap in waxproof paper or plastic wrap, and chill until firm. Slice into small 'patties' and keep chilled until needed for serving.
   Steam vegetables over boiling water until just cooked but still crunchy. Serve immediately, topped with garlic butter slices.
Serves 4

Notes
● *Any selection of young vegetables may be used. Try to achieve a variety of colours, shapes and textures, for example:*
   baby marrows, cauliflower florets, carrots.
● *For slimmers, serve steamed vegetables without garlic butter slices.*
● *For a super salad variation on this recipe, steam vegetables as described, and chill. Add 100 g button mushrooms, left whole and washed well.*
   Do not make garlic butter slices, but use the following dressing instead. Whisk four large eggs until creamy and fluffy. Whisk in 15 ml prepared mustard. Gradually beat in first 60 ml olive oil, and then 125 ml lemon juice, and lastly 60 ml cream. Season with 2 ml salt and stir over boiling water until dressing thickens. Cool and pour over vegetables.
   Both salad and dressing can be made in advance and assembled just before serving.

Orange custard

2 oranges
125 ml sugar
300 ml warm milk
2 eggs

Grate rind of 1 orange thinly and reserve. Dissolve sugar in milk. Beat eggs well and combine with milk mixture. Add grated orange rind and pour custard into a greased 1 litre soufflé mould. Bake in a pan of hot water in a pre-heated oven at 150°C for 1 hour. Remove and chill. Peel oranges completely, removing all pith and membranes, and separate into segments. Drain segments well and arrange on top of custard. Serve immediately.
Serves 4

Notes
● *Add 10 ml Van der Hum liqueur to the milk, if desired.*
● *Orange custard may be prepared up to 24 hours in advance and refrigerated until needed.*

EXECUTIVE EATING

A working lunch tends to be sandwiches and coffee – for something far more appetising and eye-catching, serve the **Working lunch** menu or the **Board lunch** menu. What to take to work for lunch is always a problem if you're watching your weight, but the **Slimmer's packed lunch** menus solve the problem with tasty low-kilojoule dishes. If you're a pasta addict, try the delectably light **Pasta special** menu – it's great for a light supper too, and there's a slimmers' variation for the weight-conscious.

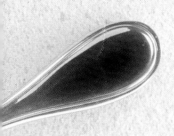

Pitta bread with feta and olive salad filling

Lamb and salad filling

8 butter lettuce leaves
125 ml cooked chickpeas
125 ml cooked lentils
300 g cold roast lamb, slivered
40 ml prepared French mustard
5 ml curry powder
8 cherry tomatoes, chopped

Line pitta pocket with lettuce. Combine chickpeas, lentils and lamb. Mix mustard and curry powder and combine with lamb mixture. Pile on lettuce and top with tomatoes.
Serves 4

Notes
● *To cook chickpeas, soak overnight in water to cover. Place in a saucepan, just cover with water and bring to boil. Simmer for 45 minutes, or until just tender.*
● *To cook lentils, soak overnight in water to cover. Place in a saucepan, just cover with water and bring to boil. Simmer for 25-30 minutes, or until just tender.*
● *Pack pitta bread and filling separately in spillproof containers and assemble just before eating.*

Feta and olive salad filling

8 young spinach leaves
60 g feta cheese, crumbled
60 g Rosetta or Drakensberg cheese, cubed
12 olives, stoned and chopped
½ English cucumber, chopped
4 cherry tomatoes, sliced
50 ml natural yoghurt
2 small cloves garlic, crushed
salt and freshly ground black pepper

Line pitta pocket with spinach leaves. Combine feta cheese with Rosetta or Drakensberg cheese, olives and cucumber and pile on top of spinach. Top with tomato slices. Combine yoghurt, garlic, salt and pepper and spoon on top of tomato.
Serves 4

Wheat beer

250 ml whole-kernel wheat
250 ml brown sugar
6-10 raisins
5 ml active dried yeast
1,5 litres lukewarm water

Soak wheat for 24 hours in cold water to cover. Drain and discard water. Add sugar, raisins, yeast and lukewarm water to wheat, mix well and leave, covered, for 24 hours. Strain and bottle. Use within 2-3 days.
Makes 1,5 litres

Note
● *Bottle beer in 375 ml bottles to make it easier to transport.*

> ### Working lunch
>
> (Menu for 4)
>
> Pitta bread
>
> Lamb and salad filling
>
> Feta and olive salad filling
>
> Wheat beer

Pitta bread

180-250 ml warm water
1 x 10 g packet active dried yeast
15 ml sugar
320 g bread flour
5 ml salt
5 ml sunflower oil

Combine 60 ml warm water with yeast and sugar and stir to dissolve. Leave in a warm place for 5 minutes, or until bubbly. Sift flour and salt into a bowl, add oil and then yeast mixture and beat until well-mixed. Add enough water to make dough form a ball. Turn out onto a floured surface and knead until smooth and elastic (5-8 minutes). Allow to rise, covered, until doubled in size (45-60 minutes). Punch down, divide into 12 pieces and roll each into a ball. Roll each ball out thinly on a lightly floured surface to a circle 15 cm in diameter. Place on lightly greased baking sheets and leave in a warm place, covered, for 25 minutes. Bake in a pre-heated oven at 200°C for 7-8 minutes, or until puffed and golden. Cool on a wire rack. To serve, cut in half (across the circle) and carefully split open to form a pocket. Fill with lamb and salad filling* or feta and olive salad filling* just before serving.
Makes 12 circles or 24 'pockets'

Note
● *Pitta bread may be stored in an airtight container or stacked, with buttered paper in between the pockets, and frozen. To serve, heat at 160°C. If stored, however, it will lose its puffiness and freshness.*

Board lunch

(Menu for 4)

Gazpacho ice

Lemon duck

Rosemary potato balls

Hot buttered lettuce and peas

Tropical fruits with kiwi fruit purée

Chilled white wine

Gazpacho ice

30 ml gelatine
60 ml dry white wine
500 g ripe tomatoes, skinned, seeded and chopped
100 ml peeled, seeded and finely chopped cucumber
    (±5 thick slices)
100 ml seeded and finely chopped red sweet pepper
    (±¼ pepper)
60 ml minced mild onion (±1 small onion)
30 ml olive or sunflower oil
5 ml salt
1 clove garlic, crushed
5 ml cayenne pepper
paper-thin cucumber slices for garnish

Soften gelatine in wine in a small saucepan for 5 minutes, then heat over low heat, stirring, until gelatine has dissolved. Purée in a blender or food processor with remaining ingredients, except cucumber slices. Freeze in freezer container for 1-2 hours or until frozen, then beat until smooth but still frozen in a food processor or blender. Working quickly, scoop mounds of gazpacho ice onto a metal tray lined with plastic wrap. Cover with foil and freeze for at least 1 hour, but preferably overnight. Soak cucumber slices in iced water for 15 minutes. Soften gazpacho ices slightly at room temperature. Drain cucumber slices and pat dry. Arrange on 4 chilled individual serving dishes and top with gazpacho ices. Serve immediately.
Serves 4

Notes
● *Gazpacho ices may be made up to 2 days in advance and stored, covered, in the freezer until needed.*
● *For a refreshing cold soup, leave out the gelatine and substitute 1 thick slice crustless fresh white bread. Place bread in blender or food processor with remaining ingredients (well-chilled), except garnish. Blend until smooth and chill well.*

Lemon duck

1 x 2 kg duck, cut into portions
lemon slices for garnish
chopped fresh parsley for garnish

Marinade
15 ml grated lemon rind
65 ml fresh lemon juice
1 clove garlic, crushed
5 ml dried thyme
2 ml salt
2 ml freshly ground black pepper

Combine marinade ingredients and marinate duck portions in it for 3-4 hours, turning often. Drain duck and discard marinade. Place duck portions in a baking dish and bake in a preheated oven at 190°C for 25 minutes, or until tender. Serve garnished with lemon slices and parsley.
Serves 4

Gazpacho ice with cucumber

Rosemary potato balls

1 kg potatoes
30 ml butter
30 ml sunflower or olive oil
10 ml chopped fresh rosemary
salt and freshly ground pepper

Peel potatoes and place them in a bowl of cold water. Using a 1 cm diameter melon ball cutter, cut out balls from potatoes, reserving scraps for another use. Simmer potato balls in boiling salted water for 5-6 minutes or until just tender. Drain well and pat dry. Heat butter and oil in a frying pan over medium heat until foam subsides. Sauté potato balls with rosemary, and salt and pepper to taste, turning for 3 minutes or until golden.
Serves 4

Notes
● *Potato balls, called Parisienne potatoes, are available from some supermarkets.*
● *Other herbs, such as dill, tarragon or marjoram, could be used in place of rosemary.*

Hot buttered lettuce and peas

350 g cos lettuce, coarsely chopped (±2 lettuces)
350 ml fresh or frozen petit pois
50 ml melted butter
salt and freshly ground black pepper

Steam lettuce and peas until just tender (about 5 minutes). Toss in melted butter and season with salt and pepper. Serve hot.
Serves 4

Tropical fruits with kiwi fruit purée

3 ripe fibreless mangoes, peeled, stoned and sliced
350 g sultana grapes, halved

Kiwi fruit purée
4 ripe kiwi fruit, peeled and chopped
juice of 1 lemon
30 ml water
30 ml sugar

Chill fruit for 30 minutes. Meanwhile, blend the purée ingredients until smooth in a food processor or blender. Arrange mango slices and sultana grapes on a serving platter and drizzle purée over them.
Serves 4-6

Notes
● *Use 1 medium pawpaw if mangoes are unavailable or out of season.*
● *If kiwi fruit is unavailable, use fresh or canned apricots instead.*
● *Kiwi fruit purée may be made in advance and refrigerated until needed. Leave at room temperature for a few minutes before pouring over chilled fruit.*

Heat oil in a saucepan and sauté onions until transparent (about 5 minutes). Add remaining ingredients, except parsley, and season to taste with salt and pepper. Simmer, covered, for 30 minutes. Allow to cool, then chill overnight. Pack separately from crispbread. Serve heaped on slices of crispbread, garnished with parsley.
Serves 6

Notes
● *Ratatouille will keep well in the refrigerator for 2-3 days. Alternatively, store serving portions in the freezer until needed.*
● *Pack in spillproof container to take to work.*

Lemon dill chicken breasts

6 chicken breasts, skinned
dill sprigs for garnish

Lemon dill sauce
50 ml gin
finely grated rind of 2 lemons
100 ml chicken stock
125ml chopped fresh dill
50 ml natural yoghurt

Heat gin to just below boiling point, add lemon rind and infuse overnight. Heat a non-stick frying pan and pack chicken breasts in it in a single layer. Cook on one side only for 5-8 minutes. Remove from pan and keep hot. Add lemon-flavoured gin and stock to pan and stir. Add dill and reduce sauce until syrupy. Stir in yoghurt. Sliver chicken breasts, pour sauce over and chill. Serve garnished with dill sprigs.
Serves 6

Slimmer's packed lunch (1)

(Menu for 1)

Chilled ratatouille

Crispbread

Lemon dill chicken breasts

Fresh fruit

Iced mineral water with lemon

Chilled ratatouille

20 ml olive or sunflower oil
2 onions, chopped
2 cloves garlic, crushed
4 baby marrows, thickly sliced
2 medium brinjals, peeled and cubed
2 green peppers, seeded and chopped
100 g black olives (optional)
2 bay leaves
5 ml chopped fresh thyme
15 ml chopped fresh basil
250 ml skinned and chopped tomatoes ($\pm$2 large tomatoes)
salt and freshly ground black pepper
chopped fresh parsley for garnish

New potato salad

100 g new potatoes (±6 potatoes)
2 ml chopped fresh dill
5 ml fresh lemon juice
5 ml olive oil
6-8 cocktail tomatoes
50 g button mushrooms (±6-8 mushrooms)

Boil potatoes in their jackets until just tender but not mushy. Halve potatoes (still in jackets) and place in a bowl. Sprinkle with dill, lemon juice and olive oil, and toss lightly to coat. Allow to cool, then pack into a container with tomatoes and mushrooms, and seal.
Serves 1

Coarse fish pâté

125 g cooked boned white fish
45 ml smooth or chunky cottage cheese with herbs
15 ml low-fat natural yoghurt
salt and freshly ground black pepper

Flake fish and combine with cottage cheese and yoghurt. Season to taste and pack into a container with a close-fitting lid.
Serves 1

Chilled orange and grapefruit segments

½ orange, peeled, segmented and with membranes removed
½ grapefruit, peeled, segmented and with membranes removed

Pack orange and grapefruit segments into a container, with juices, and seal. Refrigerate.
Serves 1

Notes
● *For a touch of luxury, add a dash of Campari before chilling.*
● *Citrus is delicious served with low-fat natural yoghurt.*
● *All of these recipes can be prepared the night before and refrigerated.*

From left: **Chilled ratatouille, lemon dill chicken breasts, crispbreads with ratatouille, iced mineral water with lemon**

Pasta special

(Menu for 4)

Pepper salad with orzo and salami

Salmon trout fettuccini with saffron butter sauce

Tomato, mozzarella and basil salad

Ripe figs

Chianti or light red wine

Salmon trout fettuccini with saffron butter sauce

500 ml shelled fresh young peas or frozen petit pois
350 g fettuccini
65 ml butter, cut into pieces
salt and freshly ground pepper
750 g smoked salmon trout, cut into cubes

Saffron butter sauce
1 ml crumbled saffron threads
30 ml minced spring onions (±2 spring onions)
30 ml white wine vinegar
45 ml dry white wine
45 ml thick cream
salt and freshly ground pepper
250 ml butter, cut into 16 pieces

Cook fresh peas in boiling salted water for 3-6 minutes, or frozen peas for 3-4 minutes, or until just tender. Drain well and set aside. Cook fettuccini in 4-5 litres boiling salted water, stirring occasionally, until just tender (7-9 minutes). Drain well and transfer to a large frying pan. Add butter, peas, and pepper to taste and cook over low heat, tossing well, until hot. Add salmon trout and cook over low heat until heated through.

Meanwhile, make sauce. Combine saffron, spring onions, vinegar and wine in a small heavy saucepan and bring to a simmer. Continue simmering, uncovered, over medium heat until reduced to about 30 ml. Stir in cream and simmer, whisking occasionally, until liquid is reduced to about 30 ml. Season with salt and pepper, reduce heat to low and whisk in butter, 1 piece at a time, lifting pan from heat occasionally to cool mixture and adding each new piece of butter before the previous one has melted completely. (Sauce should not get hot enough to liquefy.) Remove from heat and adjust seasoning if necessary. Add sauce to frying pan and toss mixture over medium heat until heated through and well-combined. Do not allow to boil. Serve immediately.
Serves 4-6

Note
● *For slimmers, instead of salmon trout fettuccini serve Fettuccini and asparagus in mushroom sauce:*
Sauté 30 ml finely chopped spring onions in 20 ml sunflower oil or butter until transparent. Add 125 ml dry white wine and bring to boil. Add 250 ml chicken stock, 100 g slivered brown mushrooms, salt and freshly ground black pepper to taste and bring back to boil. Simmer, uncovered, until reduced to 200 ml. Add 250 ml low-fat natural yoghurt mixed to a paste with 10 ml cornflour. Bring to just boiling, then simmer, stirring occasionally, for 8-10 minutes or until a coating consistency is reached. Season. Cook 250 g trimmed and chopped fresh green asparagus in boiling salted water for 7-9 minutes, or until just tender. Drain well and transfer to a bowl. Cook 175 g fettuccini in boiling salted water until just tender (7-9 minutes). Toss sauce with drained fettuccini and asparagus and serve hot.
Serves 3-4

Pepper salad with orzo and salami

Pepper salad with orzo and salami

1 large green pepper, seeded and quartered
thinly sliced radishes for garnish
4 spring onions, trimmed, for garnish

Stuffing
10 ml white wine vinegar
salt and freshly ground pepper
20 ml olive oil
100 ml orzo (rice-shaped pasta)
4 thick slices salami, cubed
60 ml crumbled feta cheese
30 ml finely chopped spring onions
    (±2 spring onions)

First make stuffing. Whisk vinegar and salt and pepper to taste in a small bowl. Add oil and whisk until well-combined. Boil orzo in a saucepan of boiling salted water until just tender (10-12 minutes). Drain, refresh under cold water and drain well in a sieve. Combine orzo with salami, feta cheese and spring onion, and season to taste with salt and pepper. Whisk oil and vinegar mixture again, then add to orzo mixture and toss well. Divide mixture among pepper quarters, top each with radish slices and arrange on a serving dish. Place spring onions between stuffed pepper quarters. Serve cold.
Serves 4

Notes
● *The stuffing may be prepared an hour or two in advance and chilled until needed.*
● *The stuffing may be used to fill cooked whole young gem squash, or piled on chicory or lettuce leaves and served as a salad.*

Tomato, mozzarella and basil salad

2 large ripe tomatoes, skinned and thickly sliced
8 thin slices mozzarella cheese, halved
125 ml finely chopped fresh basil

Dressing
30 ml olive or sunflower oil
15 ml lemon juice
salt and freshly ground black pepper
1 clove garlic, crushed

Arrange tomato slices in overlapping circles on a flat serving dish. Arrange mozzarella slices in a circle over them and sprinkle with basil. Combine and shake dressing ingredients well in a screw-top jar and drizzle over salad just before serving.
Serves 4

> **Ripe figs**
> Pile unpeeled figs on a serving dish lined with vine leaves, or peel figs, place them in a serving dish and drizzle Amaretto liqueur or port over them.

SUPER SUPPERS

Keep it simple and fuss-free for a casual supper everyone will enjoy. Savour the dishes on the **After-theatre supper** menu while you relax after a visit to the theatre. To make life even easier, try one of the two **One-dish supper** menus – each easy to prepare, light and luscious to eat. The **Pizza dinner** menu allows you to choose your own combination of toppings for a meal that's just to your taste, while the **Slimmers' supper** menu offers temptingly un-dietlike delights . . . which are nevertheless well-balanced nutritionally and low in kilojoules. And on a blustery rainy night, what could be better than settling down in front of the fire and tucking into the warming repast of the **Fireside supper**?

After-theatre supper

(Menu for 4)

Spinach and nut roulade

Seafood-stuffed croissants

White chocolate mousses

Coffee

Cognac

Spinach and nut roulade

Roulade
30 ml butter or margarine
1 onion, finely chopped
250 g spinach, trimmed and stems removed
30 ml chopped fresh parsley
salt and freshly ground black pepper
freshly grated nutmeg
4 eggs
100 ml cake flour

Stuffing
250 g chunky cottage cheese
45 ml chopped spring onions (±2 spring onions)
65 ml very finely chopped almonds or pine kernels

Grease and line a 35 x 25 cm swiss roll pan with waxproof paper. Melt butter or margarine in a saucepan and sauté onion until transparent (about 5 minutes). Add spinach and cook over high heat, stirring frequently, until no moisture remains. Remove from heat, stir in parsley, salt, pepper and nutmeg. Chop mixture finely with a sharp knife or process in a food processor. Cool. Beat eggs with a little salt until thick and creamy. Fold in spinach mixture, then flour. Turn mixture into prepared swiss roll pan and smooth out the surface. Bake in a pre-heated oven at 200°C for 10 minutes, or until firm. Turn out onto waxproof paper and carefully roll up like a swiss roll. Leave to cool while making stuffing.

Combine stuffing ingredients well. Carefully unroll roulade, remove paper and spread roulade with stuffing mixture. Roll up again and serve hot or cold, sliced.
Serves 4-6

Note
• *Prepare roulade a few hours in advance and either reheat for 10 minutes in a pre-heated oven at 100°C (to serve warm) or serve cold.*

Steam the hake for 10-15 minutes, and the shelled prawns for 5-10 minutes. Cube the hake. Allow to cool. Heat croissants through at 220°C in a pre-heated oven for 5-10 minutes. Meanwhile, combine filling ingredients. Split croissants and place bases on each of 4 plates. Spoon filling over and close with top half. Garnish with butter lettuce leaves and tomatoes, and serve. *Serves 4*

Note
● *Make seafood filling for croissants a few hours in advance and chill until ready to serve.*

Seafood-stuffed croissants

4 croissants
4 butter lettuce leaves
4 cherry tomatoes

Filling
2 spring onions, trimmed and sliced
75 g mushrooms, sliced
100 ml low-fat natural yoghurt or smooth cottage cheese
1 clove garlic, crushed
salt and freshly ground black pepper
125 g hake or monkfish fillets
125 g prawns or shrimps, shelled
125 g canned smoked mussels, drained

White chocolate mousses (top),
seafood-stuffed croissants,
spinach and nut roulade (right front)

White chocolate mousses

100 g white chocolate, broken into pieces
3 eggs, separated
250 ml thick cream
15 ml castor sugar
15 ml brandy
milk chocolate leaves for decoration

Melt chocolate in a heatproof bowl over hot (not boiling) water, then allow to cool to room temperature. Beat egg whites until stiff, then lightly whip cream and sugar together. Beat egg yolks very lightly and stir into melted chocolate. Add brandy and mix until smooth. Fold a little beaten egg white into the chocolate mixture, then fold the chocolate mixture into rest of the egg whites. Fold in cream, then spoon into 4 glass bowls or milk chocolate cases. Chill for at least 2 hours before serving. Serve decorated with dark or milk chocolate leaves.
Serves 4

Note
● *White chocolate mousses may be made up to 12 hours in advance and chilled until needed.*

Casserole of asparagus and chicken-stuffed ham rolls

8 fresh asparagus spears, steamed, or 8 canned spears,
    drained
4 chicken breast fillets, cooked and halved
16 thin slices cooked ham
125 ml fresh or frozen petit pois
100 g young green beans, chopped
200 g young carrots, chopped (±4-6 carrots)
250 g button mushrooms, chopped
30 ml butter
125 ml grated Parmesan cheese
30 ml finely chopped fresh parsley or mint

Yoghurt sauce
250 ml natural yoghurt
15 ml cornflour
125 g smooth cottage cheese
65 ml hot chicken or vegetable stock
30 ml chopped fresh parsley or mint
10 ml dill seeds
1 clove garlic, crushed
salt and freshly ground pepper

Wrap asparagus spears and chicken in ham slices and secure with toothpicks. Layer in a greased ovenproof dish. Steam peas, carrots and beans until just tender (about 5 minutes). Sprinkle over ham rolls. Sauté mushrooms in 15 ml butter until softened (about 5 minutes). Spoon over ham rolls.
    To make sauce, blend yoghurt and cornflour and place, with other ingredients, in a food processor or blender. Blend until smooth, seasoning to taste with salt and pepper, and pour over ham rolls.
    Combine Parmesan cheese and parsley or mint and sprinkle over top. Dot with remaining butter and bake, covered, in a pre-heated oven at 180°C for 15 minutes or until sauce is bubbling. Remove lid of casserole and brown topping under a hot grill. Serve immediately, with Melba toast.
Serves 4

Melba toast

8 thin slices stale white bread

Remove crusts from bread and place on a baking sheet. Place in a pre-heated oven at 180°C and bake until toasted and golden (5-10 minutes).
Serves 4

Note
● *Melba toast may be made a day or two in advance and stored in an airtight container until needed.*

Cinnamon coffee

1 litre black filter coffee
sugar to taste
2 sticks cinnamon

Make coffee to desired strength and pour into a saucepan. Add sugar to taste and cinnamon and bring to boil. Discard cinnamon before serving.
Serves 4

Note
● *Cinnamon coffee tastes best if served black, but milk may be added if you prefer.*

Marinated fish salad

500 g hake fillets, cut into very thin strips
1 green pepper, seeded and cut into strips
½ Chinese cabbage, shredded
200 ml mangetouts (optional)
8 cherry tomatoes, chopped
2 onions, cut into eighths
250 ml bean sprouts
3 carrots, grated
375 g crayfish, cooked and cut into chunks

Marinade
75 ml fresh lime or lemon juice
10 ml sunflower oil
2 ml sesame oil (optional)
6 slices fresh ginger

Dressing
75 ml fresh lime or lemon juice
30 ml sunflower oil
1 clove garlic, crushed
15 ml soy sauce
5 ml chilli sauce (optional)
5 ml brown sugar

Combine marinade ingredients and marinate fish strips in it overnight in the refrigerator. Drain and discard marinade. Combine fish with vegetables and crayfish in a large salad bowl. Blend dressing ingredients well. Add to salad, toss to combine and serve with crusty French bread.
Serves 4

Marinated fish salad with
crusty French bread

Wholewheat pizza base

125 ml wholewheat flour
125 ml white bread flour
5 ml instant dried yeast
5 ml sugar
2 ml salt
75 ml warm water
10 ml butter or margarine

Combine flours and add instant dried yeast, sugar and salt. Gradually add warm water, while kneading. Knead dough until smooth and elastic. Knead butter or margarine in, bit by bit. Leave to rise until doubled in bulk (about 30 minutes). Punch down and knead lightly. Press into a 20 cm metal pizza pan. Add desired toppings and bake in a pre-heated oven at 200°C for about 10-15 minutes, or until base is crisp and topping is cooked through. Serve hot, in slices.
Makes 1 large pizza base

Notes
● *Double quantities and freeze half, after dough has risen, for later use. To use, thaw dough and press into a pizza pan.*
● *Pizza base may be made in advance, ready for toppings to be added, and stored, covered, at room temperature until needed.*

Shortcrust pizza base

250 g cake flour
2 ml salt
175 g butter or margarine
75 ml iced water
15 ml fresh lemon juice

Sift dry ingredients together. Rub butter or margarine into flour mixture until it resembles coarse crumbs. Sprinkle water and lemon juice over and press lightly together. Wrap in wax-proof paper and chill for 30 minutes. Roll out on a lightly floured board and press into a 22 cm metal or ceramic pizza pan. Add desired toppings* and bake in a pre-heated oven at 180°C for 10-15 minutes or until base is crisp and topping is cooked through. Serve hot, in slices.
Makes 1 large pizza base

Shortcrust pizza with (clockwise from top right) onion, basil, mushroom, mozzarella cheese, baby marrow and sautéed brinjal topping; artichoke, salami, feta cheese and oregano topping; garlic, bacon and rosemary topping; smoked oyster, prawn, ricotta cheese and basil topping

Tangy tomato sauce

25 ml butter or margarine
1 onion, finely chopped
1 clove garlic, crushed
500 g ripe tomatoes, skinned and chopped
2 sprigs fresh thyme
5 ml chopped fresh parsley
2 ml chopped fresh tarragon
1 ml sugar
5 ml salt
2 ml freshly ground black pepper

Melt butter or margarine and sauté onion and garlic for 2 min-utes. Stir in remaining ingredients and simmer over low heat until thick.
Makes about 200 ml

Note
● *This sauce can be made in larger quantities and frozen, in serving portions, until needed.*

Herb-poached vegetable salad

250 g button mushrooms
250 g young green beans, topped and tailed
250 g young carrots, cut into julienne strips
    (±4-6 small carrots)
3 spring onions, trimmed and chopped

Dressing
250 ml dry white wine
250 ml water
75 ml olive or vegetable oil
juice of 2 lemons
large bunch fresh parsley
2 ml fresh thyme
1 ml fennel seeds
1 bay leaf
2 ml lightly crushed black peppercorns
2 ml lightly crushed coriander seeds
7 ml salt

First make dressing. Combine all ingredients in a saucepan and bring to boil. Reduce heat and simmer, covered, for 30 min-utes. Strain through a fine sieve and return liquid to saucepan. Add vegetables and simmer, covered, for 10-15 minutes or until vegetables are tender. Remove vegetables with a slotted spoon and keep warm. Boil liquid in a saucepan over high heat, un-covered, until reduced by half. Pour over cooked vegetables and toss to coat. Serve hot or cold.
Serves 4-6

Note
● *If serving salad cold, it may be prepared up to 6 hours in advance and chilled until needed.*

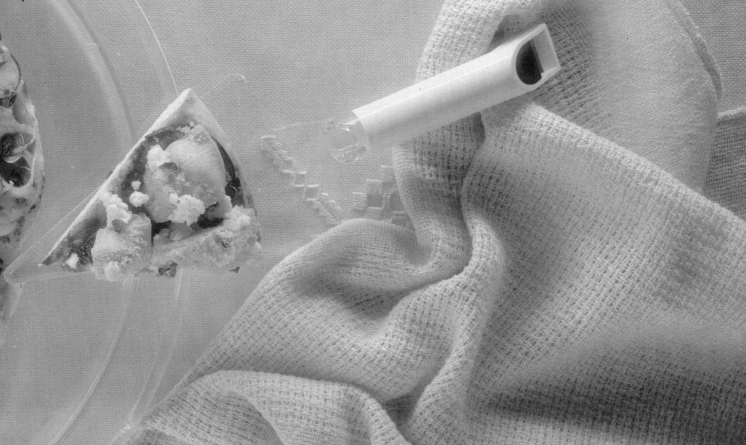

Slimmers' supper

(Menu for 2)

Spinach gnocchi

Green bean, pea and
mushroom salad with bacon

Fresh fruit, yoghurt and granola parfait

Rooibos tea

Spinach gnocchi

30 ml butter or margarine
325 g fresh spinach, chopped, or frozen chopped spinach
100 ml ricotta or low-fat cottage cheese
1 egg, lightly beaten
30 ml cake flour
125 ml grated Parmesan cheese
2 ml salt
2 ml freshly ground black pepper
2 litres simmering water

Melt butter or margarine in a saucepan, add spinach and cook for 2-3 minutes or until moisture has evaporated. Add ricotta or cottage cheese and cook, stirring, for a further 3-4 minutes. Spoon into a mixing bowl and add egg, flour, 25 ml of the Parmesan cheese, salt and pepper. Mix well, then chill for 1 hour. Shape mixture into balls about 5 cm in diameter. Drop into barely simmering water and cook, uncovered, for 5-8 minutes. Lift out with a slotted spoon and keep warm. Serve sprinkled with extra Parmesan cheese.
Serves 2

Note
● *If you're not counting kilojoules, serve gnocchi with warmed cream or sour cream, sprinkled with Parmesan cheese.*

Green bean, pea and mushroom salad with bacon

2 rashers streaky bacon
125 g young green beans, topped and tailed
15 ml sunflower oil
125 g brown mushrooms, sliced
juice of ½ lemon
salt and freshly ground black pepper
200 ml fresh or frozen petit pois, thawed

Grill bacon until crisp, drain on absorbent paper and crumble. Steam beans for 4-5 minutes, or until barely tender. Drain and cool. Heat oil in a frying pan and sauté mushrooms for 2-3 minutes. Transfer to a salad bowl. Add lemon juice, salt and pepper to taste, then stir in beans and peas. Allow to cool, then sprinkle bacon over and serve.
Serves 2

Fresh fruit, yoghurt and Granola parfait

2 ripe apricots, halved, skinned, stoned and chopped
125 ml chopped ripe pawpaw or mango
250 ml Granola
250 ml low-fat natural yoghurt
30 ml toasted flaked almonds

Opposite: **Green bean, pea and mushroom salad with bacon** (top), spinach gnocchi
Right: Fresh fruit, yoghurt and Granola parfait

Layer ingredients in 2 parfait glasses or individual glass bowls in the following order: apricots, half the Granola, half the yoghurt, pawpaw or mangoes, remaining Granola, remaining yoghurt. Top with toasted flaked almonds and chill for 30 minutes before serving.
Serves 2

Notes
● *Use soaked and stewed dried apricots or apricots canned in fruit juice if fresh ones are unavailable.*
● *Fresh fruit, yoghurt and Granola parfait may be made up to 2 hours in advance.*
● *Instead of apricots and pawpaws, try fresh figs and kiwi fruit, or apples.*
● *Dried fruits can be used if no fresh fruit is available. Soak for 1 hour or stew in a little juice.*

Buttered noodles

200 g ribbon noodles
boiling salted water
butter

Cook ribbon noodles in boiling salted water until just done
(8-12 minutes). Drain, toss in butter and serve immediately
with baked veal.
Serves 4

Note
● *For slimmers, serve without butter.*

Fireside supper

(Menu for 4)

Baked veal with oregano and tomatoes

Buttered noodles

Cos lettuce with French dressing
and herbed croûtons

Peaches with fresh mango sauce

Hot spiced orange tea

Baked veal with oregano and tomato

8 thin veal schnitzels
30 ml cake flour
30 ml sunflower oil
5 ml salt
1 ml freshly ground black pepper
8 ripe cherry tomatoes, skinned
8 small whole onions
250 ml dry red wine or chicken stock
2 bay leaves
15 ml chopped fresh oregano or 5 ml dried oregano
chopped parsley for garnish

Filling
50 ml chopped onion (±1 small onion)
50 ml chopped brinjal (±½ small brinjal)
30 ml sunflower oil
125 ml fresh wholewheat breadcrumbs
1 ml salt
pinch freshly ground black pepper
1 clove garlic, chopped
125 ml finely skinned chopped ripe tomatoes
pinch brown sugar
30 ml finely chopped walnuts or pecan nuts (optional)
15 ml chopped fresh oregano or 5 ml dried oregano

First make filling. Sauté onions and brinjals in heated oil until
lightly browned. Add remaining ingredients, moistening with
a little wine or stock if mixture is too dry. Spoon a little filling
mixture onto each schnitzel, roll up and secure with string or
toothpicks. Dust with flour. Brown meat parcels on both sides
in heated oil in a casserole dish. Season with salt and pepper.
Insert cherry tomatoes and small onions between veal rolls.
Heat wine or stock to lukewarm with bay leaves and oregano
and pour over veal. Cover and bake in a pre-heated oven at
160°C for 1-1¼ hours or until meat is tender. Remove string or
toothpicks and sprinkle with parsley just before serving with buttered noodles.
Serves 4

Cos lettuce with French dressing and herbed
croûtons, baked veal with oregano
and tomato on a bed of buttered noodles (front)

Cos lettuce with French dressing and herbed croûtons

1 small cos lettuce, separated into leaves

Dressing
50 ml sunflower or olive oil
15 ml lemon juice
5 ml cider vinegar
2 ml salt
freshly ground black pepper

Herbed croûtons
2 slices day-old white bread
20 ml butter
5 ml chopped fresh mixed herbs
30 ml sunflower oil

Place lettuce leaves in a salad bowl. Combine dressing ingredients well and toss with lettuce.

To make croûtons, remove crusts from bread, combine butter with herbs and spread on bread. Cube bread and fry lightly on all sides in heated sunflower oil (about 1 minute). Add to salad and toss lightly before serving.
Serves 4

Note
● *Herbed croûtons may be made up to 24 hours in advance. Crisp again, if necessary, in the oven before using.*

Peaches with fresh mango sauce

375 ml water
45 ml clear honey
4 ripe Kakamas or yellow cling peaches, thinly peeled, halved and stoned
15 ml Kirsch
2 large ripe fibreless mangoes, peeled and stoned
2 mint sprigs for decoration

Combine water and honey in a saucepan over low heat. Add peach halves and poach over medium heat for 10-12 minutes, or until peaches are just tender. Remove peaches from heat and slice. Transfer, with poaching liquid, to a glass bowl and sprinkle with Kirsch. Cool to room temperature, then chill for 30 minutes. To make sauce, chop mangoes coarsely and purée. Add 50 ml poaching liquid and mix well. Spoon over peaches and decorate with mint sprigs.
Serves 4

Notes
● *Use peaches canned in fruit juice if fresh ones are unavailable. Drain peaches and poach in water and honey for 5 minutes.*
● *Peaches may be prepared the day before and refrigerated. Purée mangoes just before serving.*

Hot spiced orange tea

4 sachets honey-flavoured rooibos tea
1 stick cinnamon
1 piece fresh ginger, bruised
3 cloves
750 ml boiling water
orange slices

Bring all ingredients except orange slices to boil in a saucepan. Strain into a glass teapot, adding orange slices. Serve hot.
Serves 4

Note
● *Glass mugs in silver or basketware holders are ideal for serving hot spiced orange tea in.*

WINTER WARMERS

*W*hat could be more comforting on a shivering winter's night than a bowl of steaming hot soup? The **Soup supper** menu gives you a choice of two, both of them guaranteed to satisfy, with savoury breadsticks as the perfect complement. For a totally different focus, try the **Kebab grill** menu – sizzling morsels of chicken and vegetables, accompanied by crunchy spinach salad with croûtons, and finishing off with fruity baked apples and mulled wine to keep out the chill. Country folk know the value of fragrant, piping hot stews, and the **Bistro fare** menu and the **French country cooking** menu offer the best of French provincial cooking brought right up to date with lighter but still flavoursome ingredients.

Soup supper

(Menu for 4)

Curried squash soup

OR

Vegetable soup with frikkadels

Rosemary breadsticks

Fresh fruit

Filter coffee

Curried squash soup

1 kg yellow gem squash
1 large onion, chopped
50 ml chopped celery (±1 stalk)
1 Granny Smith apple, peeled, cored and chopped
30 ml butter
15 ml curry powder
1 litre chicken or vegetable stock
250 ml buttermilk or low-fat natural yoghurt
grated lemon rind or lemon slices for garnish

Cook gem squash, either by baking in a pre-heated oven at 180°C for 35 minutes or boiling in water until just done (about 20 minutes). Remove pips and discard. Scoop out flesh. Place onion, celery, apple and butter in a saucepan, cover tightly and leave to 'sweat' for 5 minutes over low heat. Add curry powder and sauté, stirring, for 3 minutes. Add stock and boil, covered, for 30 minutes. Add squash and boil for 5 minutes, then purée in a blender or food processor. Add buttermilk or yoghurt and heat until just warm. (Do not boil, otherwise soup will curdle.) Serve immediately, garnished with grated lemon rind or lemon slices and accompanied by rosemary breadsticks*.
Serves 4

From left: **Vegetable soup with frikkadels, rosemary breadsticks, curried squash soup**

Vegetable soup with frikkadels

1 litre chicken or veal stock
4 medium carrots, sliced
250 ml fresh green peas
½ head cauliflower, broken into florets
2 potatoes, peeled and diced
250 g green beans, sliced
1 leek, sliced
5 ml chopped fresh savory or mint for garnish

Frikkadels
250 g lean steak mince
25 ml chopped onion (±½ small onion)
1 slice white bread, soaked in milk and pressed dry
1 egg
5 ml chopped fresh parsley
2 ml salt
1 ml freshly ground black pepper
100 ml dried breadcrumbs

First make frikkadels. Combine all ingredients except breadcrumbs. Form into small balls, roll in breadcrumbs and chill while making soup.
   Heat stock in a large saucepan. Add vegetables and cook for 15 minutes. Add frikkadels and cook for a further 10 minutes. Season if necessary. Sprinkle with savory or mint and serve.
Serves 4-6

Note
● *Frikkadels may be made up to 2 hours in advance and chilled.*

Rosemary breadsticks

500 g cake flour
5 g instant dried yeast (½ x 10 g packet)
300 ml warm water
30 ml olive or sunflower oil
1 egg, beaten with 30 ml water
45 ml very finely chopped fresh rosemary
coarse salt

In a large bowl, mix 250 g (500 ml) flour with yeast, and add water. Mix until smooth. Add oil, 30 ml egg mixture (reserve remainder for glaze) and rosemary. Mix in enough remaining flour, 75 g (125 ml) at a time, to make a soft dough. Knead on a lightly floured surface until smooth and elastic – about 8 minutes. Grease a large bowl, add dough and turn dough around in it to coat surface of dough with grease. Allow to rise, covered, for 30 minutes. Divide dough in half. Roll each half into a rope 40 cm long and cut into 14 pieces. Roll each piece into a rope 30 cm long. Make breadsticks by twisting 2 ropes together, and place on a greased baking sheet. Repeat until all have been twisted. Brush with reserved egg mixture and sprinkle with coarse salt. Bake in a pre-heated oven at 200°C for 15 minutes, or until breadsticks are golden. Cool on a wire rack.
Makes 14

Note
● *Rosemary breadsticks may be made in advance and stored in an airtight container until needed.*

Chicken saté with peanut sauce

1 x 1,5 kg chicken, boned and cubed

Marinade
15 ml sunflower oil
1 large onion, finely chopped
1 clove garlic, crushed
10 ml curry powder
5 ml ground coriander
pinch cayenne pepper
pinch ground ginger
30 ml fruit chutney
salt and freshly ground black pepper
150 ml natural yoghurt

Peanut sauce
125 g chunky peanut butter
lemon juice to taste
soy sauce to taste
freshly ground black pepper
2 ml Tabasco sauce

Place chicken cubes in a large flat dish. Combine marinade ingredients and pour over chicken. Marinate for 3 hours, turning often. Thread chicken onto skewers and grill or braai until cooked (10-15 minutes), basting often with marinade.

To make peanut sauce, combine leftover marinade with peanut butter, lemon juice, soy sauce, black pepper to taste and Tabasco sauce, mixing well. Serve as a dipping sauce with chicken saté.
Serves 4

Note
● *Prepare marinade and marinate chicken in advance.*

Vegetable kebabs with garlic butter

4 large brown mushrooms, quartered
8 cherry tomatoes
8 small onions, blanched
1 small brinjal, cut into 12 chunks
4 baby mealies, halved
2 bay leaves, halved
salt and freshly ground black pepper

Garlic butter
65 ml butter
2 cloves garlic, crushed

Thread vegetables alternately onto 4 large skewers. Thread ½ bay leaf onto each skewer, between a mushroom quarter and cherry tomato. Sprinkle with salt and pepper.

To make garlic butter, mix butter and garlic, combining well. Grill or braai vegetable kebabs until cooked, basting often with garlic butter. Serve with any remaining garlic butter.
Serves 4

Notes
● *For slimmers, serve kebabs without garlic butter.*
● *Prepare vegetables for vegetable kebabs in advance, thread onto skewers and set aside, covered, until needed. The garlic butter may also be made in advance and refrigerated until needed.*

Opposite: **Chicken saté** (top), **vegetable kebabs with garlic butter, peanut sauce** (right). Above: **Spinach salad with croûtons**

Spinach salad with croûtons

12 young spinach leaves

Croûtons
sunflower oil
2 thick slices stale white bread, cubed and crusts removed

Dressing
30 ml sunflower oil
15 ml tarragon vinegar
salt and freshly ground black pepper

Trim spinach and break into bite-sized pieces. Wash well, shake dry and place in a salad bowl.

To make croûtons, heat oil in a frying pan and fry bread cubes on all sides until crisp (about 1 minute). Remove from frying pan and drain on absorbent paper. Add to spinach.

Combine dressing ingredients in a screw-top jar and shake to mix well. Just before serving, pour over spinach and toss well.
Serves 4

Baked apples with apricot, fig and nut stuffing

15 ml honey
50 ml dried figs, chopped
50 ml dried apricots, chopped
30 ml cashew nuts or walnuts, finely chopped
15 ml lemon juice
4 large Granny Smith apples, cored
65 ml unsweetened apple juice
natural yoghurt (optional)

Combine honey, figs, apricots, nuts and lemon juice in a saucepan and heat gently, stirring constantly, until well-combined. Stuff apple cavities with mixture, pressing it down firmly. Make a shallow horizontal cut around each apple. Place apples in an ovenproof dish, pour apple juice over and bake in a pre-heated oven at 180°C for 45-55 minutes, or until soft. Serve immediately, drizzled over with natural yoghurt, if desired.
Serves 4

Mulled wine

1 x 750 ml bottle dry red wine
1 lemon, sliced
300 g sugar
3 whole cloves
1 piece fresh ginger, crushed
1 piece stick cinnamon
100 ml brandy
50 ml Van der Hum liqueur
lemon slices for garnish

Bring all the ingredients except last three to boil in a saucepan. Remove from stove and leave for 1-2 hours. Discard lemon slices and spices. Heat wine to boiling point. Reduce heat, then add brandy and Van der Hum liqueur but do not boil. Serve immediately garnished with fresh lemon slices.
Makes 1 litre

Note
● *Prepare mulled wine in advance up to the point where the mixture is left to infuse. Discard spices and lemon slices and reheat wine with brandy and Van der Hum just before serving.*
● *Serve the mulled wine in heatproof glasses, preferably with handles – otherwise the drink may be too hot to hold.*

Bistro fare

(Menu for 4)

Bourride with rouille

Crusty French bread

Citrus crumble

Riesling wine

Bourride with rouille

Bourride with rouille

Bourride with rouille

50 ml olive or sunflower oil
2 onions, thinly sliced
2 leeks, thinly sliced
1 fennel bulb, thinly sliced
3 cloves garlic, crushed
4 large ripe tomatoes, skinned and chopped
1 strip orange rind, blanched
1 strip lemon rind, blanched
a few sprigs fresh thyme
3 sprigs fresh parsley
pinch saffron
1,5 litres fish stock
250 ml dry white wine
salt and freshly ground black pepper
1 kg Cape salmon, filleted, skinned and cubed
1 uncooked crayfish tail, split and cut across
16 black mussels in shells, cleaned
250 g calamari, sliced
freshly grated Parmesan cheese

Rouille
1 egg yolk
5 ml Dijon mustard (prepared)
5 ml chilli paste
3 large cloves garlic
15 ml lemon juice
15 ml olive oil
125 ml sunflower oil
salt and freshly ground black pepper

Heat oil in a large heavy-based saucepan and sauté onions, leeks and fennel until softened. Stir in crushed garlic and tomatoes. Simmer for 5-10 minutes, then add blanched orange and lemon rind, thyme, parsley and saffron. Add strained fish stock, wine, salt and pepper to taste and cook over high heat for 20 minutes, or until slightly reduced. Add Cape salmon and cook for 10 minutes. Strain and set aside cooked fish. Bring soup to boil again, add crayfish and mussels and simmer, covered, for 5 minutes. Discard any mussels that do not open. Add calamari and reserved Cape salmon and cook until calamari is opaque (about 2 minutes).

Meanwhile, prepare rouille. Blend egg yolk, mustard, chilli paste and garlic in a food processor or blender, then beat in lemon juice and oils, drop by drop, to form a thick mayonnaise. Season to taste with salt and pepper.

Serve soup garnished with Parmesan cheese, accompanied by crusty French bread spread with rouille.
Serves 4-6

Note
• *Bourride may be prepared a few hours in advance and reheated before serving.*

Citrus crumble

1 orange
1 grapefruit
1 small pineapple

Topping
125 ml brown sugar
5 ml ground ginger
125 ml rolled oats
125 ml wholewheat flour
125 ml butter
125 ml flaked almonds
125 ml chopped walnuts
250 ml natural yoghurt (optional)

Peel orange and grapefruit and slice into segments, removing all pith and seeds. Peel and slice pineapple. Layer fruit in base of an ovenproof dish. Combine sugar, ginger, oats and flour and rub in butter until mixture is crumbly. Add nuts and combine well. Spoon over fruit and bake in a pre-heated oven at 180°C for 20-30 minutes or until topping is golden brown and crisp. Serve with natural yoghurt, if desired, or egg custard.
Serves 4-6

Note
• *Citrus crumble may be made in advance and reheated at 200°C for 10 minutes.*

Veal pot au feu

30 ml sunflower oil
1 large onion, thinly sliced
500 g stewing veal, cubed
200 g small onions
200 g new potatoes
300 ml onion or vegetable stock
125 g butternut squash, peeled, seeded and cubed
    (½ butternut)
2 cloves garlic, crushed
10 ml chopped fresh tarragon, or 5 ml dried
1 bay leaf
bouquet garni
salt and freshly ground black pepper

Heat oil in a large saucepan and sauté sliced onion until golden
(5-10 minutes). Add meat and sear quickly on all sides to seal in
juices. Add remaining ingredients except seasoning. Cook,
covered, over medium heat until meat is tender and vegetables
are tender but still whole (1-1½ hours). Season to taste with salt
and pepper and, if necessary, thicken sauce with a little flour
mixed to a paste with water. Cook a further 5-10 minutes and serve.
Serves 4

Note
● *A slow cooker cooks this stew perfectly. Sauté onion and sear
meat on the stove, then transfer to the slow cooker and cook until
tender, or overnight.*

Opposite: Corn and tomato salad with herb vinaigrette (top), veal pot au feu. Above: Caramelised apple tart

Corn and tomato salad with herb vinaigrette

500 g baby mealies, lightly steamed for ±5 minutes
2 large ripe tomatoes, quartered
1 green pepper, seeded and chopped

Herb vinaigrette
30 ml sunflower oil
5 ml lemon juice
5 ml mixed chopped fresh herbs

Combine mealies, tomatoes and pepper in a bowl. Combine vinaigrette ingredients in a screw-top jar and shake to blend well. Toss with salad ingredients just before serving in individual bowls with veal pot au feu*.
Serves 4

Caramelised apple tart

250 g puff pastry*
30 ml castor sugar

Apple filling
4 Golden Delicious apples, peeled, cored and sliced
butter

Topping
5 ml honey
65 ml unsweetened apple juice
30 ml Calvados (optional)

Roll pastry out to a circle 25 cm in diameter. Use to line a pie plate. Sprinkle castor sugar on top. Arrange apple slices in overlapping circles on top of pastry and dot with butter. Bake in a pre-heated oven at 220°C for 20-30 minutes, or until apples are golden and pastry is lightly caramelised. Remove from oven. Mix honey with apple juice and Calvados and pour over apples. Serve immediately, in wedges.
Serves 4-6

Notes
• *Caramelised apple tart may be prepared in advance, without the topping. To serve, reheat tart, heat the topping and pour over tart.*
• *For a more tart filling, use Granny Smith apples instead of Golden Delicious apples.*
• *Serve with cream, if desired.*

EASY ENTERTAINING

Celebrate the return of elegant entertaining with the Fifties-style **Cocktails at 5** menu – tasty titbits to nibble on as you sip a classic cocktail with a difference! Dessert parties are all the rage, and the **Dessert party** menu gives you a flavourful selection of light, simple yet stylish puddings to serve to sweet-toothed guests (and they aren't all teenagers). The **Not-quite-vegetarian** dinner menu offers a variety of tempting dishes for those who are eating less red meat, for whatever reason, and proves that lighter eating need not be boring. Enjoy leisurely dining at its best with the **Elegant formal dinner** menu – a sumptuous spread that looks and tastes marvellous, yet isn't heavy. An easy and informal way to entertain is to invite guests to afternoon tea, and the **Afternoon tea** menu provides just the right combination of sweet and savoury delights to ensure success. Traditional Christmas fare doesn't really suit the South African climate or lifestyle, so break with tradition and serve the **Cool Christmas** menu instead. End off the year with the easiest ever way to entertain – the serve-yourself **Auld Lang Syne party** menu leaves the cook free to enjoy herself or himself and allows guests to eat whatever they prefer.

Cocktails at 5

(Menu for 8)

Steak tartare on Melba toast

Crayfish chunks with anchoiade

Spiced almonds

Ham sesame bites

Savoury cheese pasties

Batter-dipped vegetables

Watercress purée

Beetroot yoghurt purée

Rum and pineapple fizz

Amarula sidecar

Old-fashioned

Steak tartare on Melba toast

500 g extra-lean topside mince
2 ml Worcestershire sauce
2 ml Tabasco sauce
1 egg yolk
10 ml very finely chopped onion
15 ml finely chopped fresh parsley
24 small slices Melba toast*
30 ml finely chopped capers
salt and freshly ground black pepper
parsley sprigs for garnish

Process mince in a food processor until very fine. Combine with Worcestershire sauce, a few drops of Tabasco sauce, egg yolk, onion and parsley. Pile on top of Melba toast* slices just before serving and garnish with capers, salt and pepper and parsley sprigs.
Serves 8

Note
• *The meat mixture cannot be stored as it does not keep well.*

Crayfish chunks with anchoiade

4 large crayfish tails, cooked

Anchoiade
100 g anchovies in oil
2 cloves garlic
15 ml fresh basil or 5 ml dried basil
15 ml prepared French mustard
15 ml wine vinegar
2 ml dried thyme
250 ml olive oil

Remove flesh from crayfish tails and chop into chunks. Arrange around edges of a serving platter, leaving place in centre for anchoiade. To make anchoiade, combine all ingredients except olive oil in a food processor or blender and blend to form a smooth purée. Add oil slowly, with machine running. Transfer to a bowl and place bowl in centre of serving platter.
Serves 8

Spiced almonds

100 ml butter or margarine
200 g blanched almonds
salt
cayenne pepper
paprika

Heat butter or margarine in a large frying pan, add almonds and toss to coat completely. Remove from pan. Sprinkle liberally with salt, add a little cayenne pepper and paprika, and allow to cool.
Serves 8

Note
• *Spiced almonds may be made up to a week in advance and stored in an airtight container.*

Ham sesame bites

100 g cooked ham, finely diced
50 ml chopped stuffed green olives
250 g smooth cottage cheese or cream cheese
65 ml toasted sesame seeds

Combine ham, olives and cottage cheese or cream cheese, and roll into balls. Roll in sesame seeds, pressing seeds in firmly, and chill.
Serves 8

Note
• *Ham sesame bites may be made up to 12 hours in advance and refrigerated until ready to serve.*

Steak tartare on melba toast (left), spiced almonds (top), ham sesame bites

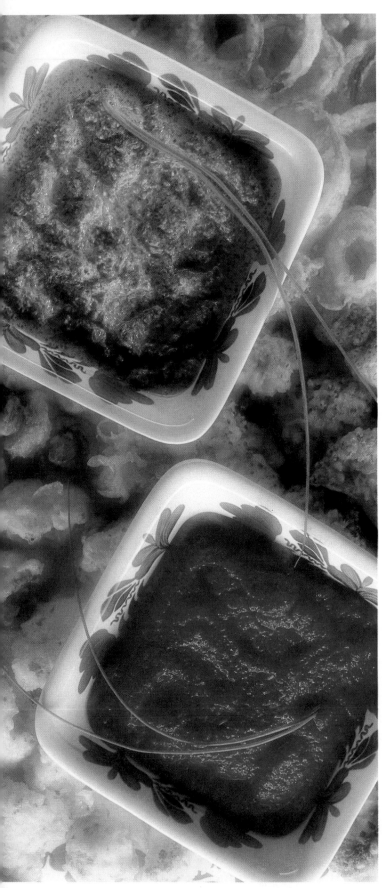

Savoury cheese pasties

400 g shortcrust pastry *

Filling
250 g chunky cottage cheese
250 g Gruyère or Cheddar cheese, grated
4 eggs
salt and freshly ground pepper
45 ml thick cream or natural yoghurt

First make filling. Combine cheeses with 3 beaten eggs, season with salt and pepper and add cream or yoghurt. Roll dough out very thinly and cut into 12 cm diameter rounds. Place 30 ml filling on each round. Fold dough over and seal, pinching edges together to seal and form pasty shapes. Stand pasties upright on folded edge on greased baking sheet. Beat remaining egg and use to brush pasties. Bake in pre-heated oven at 180 °C for 25 minutes, or until lightly browned. Serve hot.
Makes 16

Note
● *Pasties may be baked the day before and stored in an airtight container. Reheat in a pre-heated oven at 200 °C for 10 minutes.*

Batter-dipped vegetables

16 young broccoli florets
16 young cauliflower florets
16 button mushrooms
16 onion rings
sunflower oil

Batter
1 egg, beaten
1 egg yolk, beaten
175 ml water
200 ml cake flour

Combine batter ingredients to make a smooth mixture. Dip vegetable pieces in batter, a few at a time, and deep-fry very quickly in hot oil (not more than 1 minute). Drain on absorbent paper and serve immediately with watercress purée* and beetroot yoghurt purée*.
Serves 8

Note
● *Serve vegetables as soon as they come out of the pan, otherwise they will lose their crispness.*

Watercress purée

500 g watercress, trimmed
100 ml pine kernels
60 ml sunflower oil
salt and freshly ground black pepper

Purée watercress, pine kernels and oil in a food processor or blender, seasoning to taste with salt and pepper.
Makes about 500 ml

Batter-dipped vegetables with watercress purée (top) and beetroot yoghurt purée

Beetroot yoghurt purée

4 young beetroot, cooked
250 ml natural yoghurt
5 ml dill seeds
salt and freshly ground black pepper

Pureé all ingredients in a food processor or blender until smooth. Chill before serving.
Makes 500 ml

Note
● *Beetroot yoghurt purée may be made a few hours in advance and chilled until needed.*

Rum and pineapple fizz

50 ml light rum
65 ml chilled unsweetened pineapple juice
10 ml lime juice
ice-cubes
chilled soda water
lemon or lime slice for decoration

Combine rum, pineapple juice and lime juice well. Half-fill a tall glass with ice-cubes and pour rum mixture over. Top up with soda water and serve decorated with a lemon or lime slice.
Serves 1

Amarula sidecar

25 ml brandy
15 ml Amarula liqueur
10 ml lemon juice
2 ice-cubes
lemon twist for decoration

Place brandy, Amarula, lemon juice and ice in a cocktail shaker and mix. Strain into a cocktail glass and decorate with a lemon twist.
Serves 1

Note
● *Peach schnapps may be used instead of Amarula liqueur.*

Old-fashioned

1 sugar lump
dash Angostura bitters
dash soda water
2 ice-cubes
25 ml whisky
half slice orange for decoration

Put sugar lump into a glass, shake bitters on top and add soda. Stir until sugar has dissolved. Add ice-cubes and coat with dissolved sugar. Add whisky, stir and float half orange slice on top for decoration.
Serves 1

Rum and pineapple fizz (top), Amarula sidecar (centre) and an old-fashioned

Pear soufflés

3 very ripe dessert pears
600 ml water
165 ml sugar
1 vanilla bean or 2 ml vanilla essence
2 ml Kirsch or peach schnapps
2 eggs, separated
1 ml salt

Peel, quarter and core pears. Bring water, 65 ml of the sugar, and vanilla to boil and poach pears in syrup for 10-15 minutes, or until soft. Remove from syrup and purée in a blender or food processor with 100 ml sugar and Kirsch or peach schnapps. Spoon purée into a bowl with lightly beaten egg yolks, mixing well. Beat egg whites with salt until just stiff without being dry. Fold whites gently into pear mixture, spoon soufflé mixture into a 1 litre mould and bake in a pre-heated oven at 180°C for 8-10 minutes. Serve immediately.
Serves 8

Brandied prunes with sabayon sauce

32 plump dried prunes
250 ml brandy
100 ml sugar
250 ml water
3 whole cloves
1 piece stick cinnamon

Sabayon sauce
6 egg yolks
200 ml sugar
250 ml dry sparkling wine

Brandied prunes with sabayon sauce (top), crème caramel with crunchy pecan topping (centre), watermelon berry sorbet in an almond tuile

Soak prunes overnight in brandy. To make syrup, dissolve sugar in water in a saucepan, add cloves and cinnamon and boil until syrup thickens (about 10 minutes). Add prunes and brandy, and poach for 5 minutes.

To make sauce, cream together egg yolks and sugar, stirring continuously over a saucepan of hot water. Add wine, stirring. Beat sauce over warm water until thick and foamy. Serve spooned over prunes or separately.

Serves 8

Notes

● *Preserved fresh prunes may also be used. Pack 1.5 kg fresh prunes into dry sterilised jars. Heat together 150 ml sugar, 250 ml water, 8 cloves and 1 piece stick cinnamon until slightly thickened. Combine with 750 ml brandy and pour over prunes in jars. Seal and store for 3 months before use.*

● *Soak prunes in brandy overnight but sabayon sauce must be made just before serving.*

Crème caramel with crunchy pecan topping

Pecan topping
100 ml sugar
20 ml water
125 ml chopped pecan nuts

Crème caramel
500 ml milk
2 ml vanilla essence
100 g sugar
3 eggs
2 egg yolks

First make topping. Mix sugar and water in a saucepan and stir slowly and continuously over low heat until sugar has dissolved. Increase heat and allow to caramelise. Leave to cool until starting to harden. Use to coat base of a 1 litre mould, oiled or sprayed with nonstick cooking spray.

To make crème caramel, heat milk with vanilla essence to just below boiling point. Beat sugar, eggs and egg yolks together. Carefully pour hot milk into egg mixture, whisking constantly. Pour carefully into mould. Place mould in a pan of water, with the water reaching halfway up sides of mould. Bake in a preheated oven at 200°C for 20 minutes, or until set. Turn out onto a platter and top with nuts. Place briefly under a hot grill to crisp topping and serve immediately.

Serves 8

Note

● *Crème caramel may also be served cold, without topping.*

Watermelon berry sorbet

375 ml water
250 ml sugar
750 g ripe watermelon, seeded and cut into chunks
400 g ripe strawberries, hulled
30 ml crème de cassis or cherry brandy

Combine water and sugar in a saucepan. Stir over low heat until sugar dissolves, then remove from heat and cool. Purée watermelon and strawberries in a blender or food processor and stir in sugar syrup and crème de cassis or cherry brandy. Pour into freezer container and freeze until just firm. Beat well, and return to container. Repeat once, then freeze until firm. Scoop into balls and serve with almond tuiles.

Serves 8

Note

● *Watermelon berry sorbet may be prepared a few days in advance and stored in the freezer until needed.*

Almond tuiles

65 ml sugar
25 ml butter
15 ml honey
25 ml thick cream
1 ml almond essence
15 ml cake flour
100 ml flaked almonds

Combine sugar, butter, honey and cream in a small saucepan and bring to boil, stirring. Simmer, stirring, for 5 minutes. Remove from heat and mix in almond essence, flour and almonds. Let mixture cool for 2-4 minutes. (If it becomes too stiff to handle, heat carefully again.) Drop spoonfuls of mixture onto parchment-lined baking sheets and bake in a pre-heated oven at 200°C for 5-8 minutes, or until golden. For flat tuiles, leave to cool completely before removing from parchment. Otherwise shape before completely cold. Tuiles may be shaped like brandy snaps over a wooden spoon, or into cones or flutes.

Makes 12-15

Note

● *Almond tuiles may be prepared up to 2 days in advance and stored in an airtight container until needed.*

Buttermilk peach ice cream in peach halves

8 large yellow or green loose-pit peaches, peeled, halved and stoned
250 ml sugar
375 ml buttermilk
50 ml Advokaat (optional)
375 ml cream

Purée peaches with sugar in a blender or food processor. Stir in buttermilk, Advokaat and cream and pour into freezer container. Freeze until nearly firm. Beat well and refreeze. Repeat once, then freeze until firm. Serve scoops of ice cream in yellow loose-pit peach halves.

Serves 6-8

Note

● *Buttermilk peach ice cream may be made a few days in advance and frozen until needed. Thaw slightly in the refrigerator.*

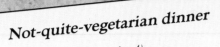

Not-quite-vegetarian dinner

(Menu for 4)

Vegetable bouillon
with egg custard rounds

Brinjal charlotte with fresh tomato sauce

Stuffed baby marrows with mint pesto

Radish and watercress salad

Stilton with port and crackers

Strawberry tulipes

Vinho verde

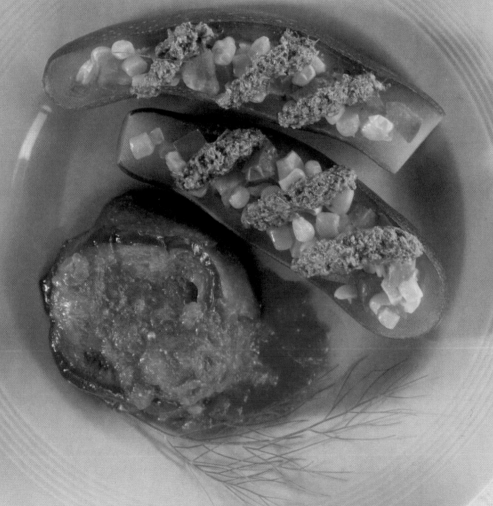

Radish and watercress salad (top),
stuffed baby marrows with
mint pesto and brinjal charlotte
with fresh tomato sauce

Vegetable bouillon with egg custard rounds

30 ml butter
30 ml olive oil
6 large carrots, diced
2 turnips, diced
1 onion, coarsely chopped
2 large leeks, coarsely chopped
4 stalks celery, coarsely chopped
2 litres water
60 g dried beans, soaked overnight
bouquet garni
5 ml sugar
10 ml salt
freshly ground black pepper
200 ml carrots, cut into julienne strips, blanched
    and refreshed for garnish
125 ml sliced leek (±1 medium leek) for garnish

Egg custard rounds
1 large egg
1 large egg yolk
125 ml milk
white pepper and salt

Melt butter in a large saucepan, add olive oil and sauté vegetables (except beans and vegetables for garnish) until they change colour (10-15 minutes). Add 250 ml water and simmer until liquid has been absorbed. Add beans and remaining water and bring to boil. Skim, then add bouquet garni, sugar, salt and pepper and simmer, covered, for 2-2½ hours. Strain through a fine sieve. Meanwhile, make egg custard rounds. Whisk egg, egg yolk, milk, pepper and salt to taste in a bowl and pour mixture into a buttered heavy 20 cm diameter round cake pan lined with buttered waxproof paper. Set pan in a deep frying pan, add enough boiling water to reach halfway up sides of cake tin and place a heavy heatproof plate on top of pan to keep it immersed in water. Cook over medium heat, keeping water at a simmer, for 15-20 minutes or until set. Remove from stove and cool for 5 minutes. Invert custard onto buttered foil, peel off paper and cut out rounds with a small biscuit cutter. Divide carrots and leeks among soup plates, pour bouillon over and serve garnished with rounds.
Serves 4-6

Note
• *Make custard rounds just before serving.*

Brinjal charlotte with fresh tomato sauce

3-4 small brinjals, trimmed and sliced
salt and freshly ground black pepper
150 ml olive or sunflower oil
1 medium onion, finely chopped
1 clove garlic, crushed
10 ripe tomatoes, skinned, seeded and chopped
300 ml natural yoghurt
150 ml chicken stock

Sprinkle brinjal slices with salt and leave for 30 minutes. Rinse with cold water and dry on absorbent paper. Heat 30 ml oil in a saucepan and sauté onion until lightly browned. Add garlic, tomatoes, salt and pepper to taste and cook, stirring occasionally, for 20-25 minutes or until mixture is thick and pulpy. Heat remaining oil in a large frying pan and brown brinjal slices on both sides. Arrange a layer of overlapping slices in the bottom and up sides of a lightly greased 1,5 litre charlotte mould or 4-6 small moulds. Reserve a third of tomato mixture for sauce. Spread a little of remainder on brinjal slices in base of mould, then spread a little yoghurt on top. Add another layer of brinjals. Continue laying brinjals, yoghurt and tomato mixture until all ingredients have been used, ending with a layer of brinjals. Mix reserved tomato mixture with stock to make a sauce. Cover mould with foil and bake in a pre-heated oven at 180°C for 45-50 minutes, or until brinjals are tender. Cool slightly, then unmould onto a serving dish. Bring tomato sauce to boil, season with salt and pepper if necessary and pour over mould. Serve hot or cold.
Serves 4-6

Note
• *If serving cold, prepare charlotte the day before and refrigerate.*

Stuffed baby marrows with mint pesto

50 ml olive or sunflower oil
500 ml whole corn kernels
2 ripe tomatoes, seeded and chopped
salt and freshly ground black pepper
4 large baby marrows

Mint pesto
750 ml tightly packed fresh mint leaves
3 small cloves garlic, crushed
200 ml chopped walnuts
75 ml grated Parmesan cheese
salt
150 ml olive or sunflower oil

First make mint pesto. Purée mint leaves, garlic, walnuts, Parmesan cheese and salt to taste in a blender or food processor. With motor running, add oil in a steady stream, blending to form a smooth mixture. Transfer pesto to a bowl, cover with plastic wrap and chill for 30 minutes.

Heat 50 ml oil in a large heavy-based frying pan and stir-fry corn for 1 minute. Add tomato and salt and pepper to taste and stir to combine. Transfer mixture to a bowl. Trim and halve baby marrows horizontally. Scoop out and discard seeds. Steam shells for 3-5 minutes, or until barely tender. Drain on absorbent paper and allow to cool. Spread 7 ml pesto in each baby marrow shell and top with corn and tomato mixture. Spoon more pesto mixture over in 3 diagonal strips, each about 1 cm wide. Serve at room temperature.
Serves 4-6

Note
• *Stuffed baby marrows with mint pesto may be prepared up to 3 hours in advance and stored, covered, at room temperature.*

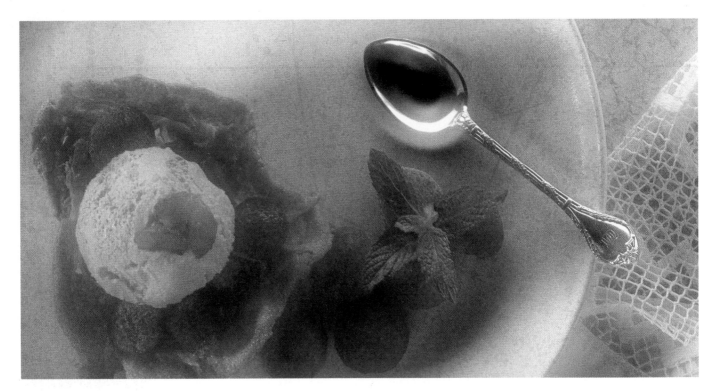

Strawberry tulipe

Radish and watercress salad

1 bunch white radishes, trimmed
1 bunch small red radishes, trimmed
500 g (±2 bunches) watercress, trimmed

Dressing
30 ml sunflower oil
10 ml lemon juice
5 ml prepared whole grain mustard
salt and freshly ground pepper

Slice radishes and place in a bowl. Add most of the watercress and toss. Chop remaining watercress very finely and set aside.
   Combine dressing ingredients in a screw-top jar and shake to mix well. Just before serving, pour over radishes and watercress, toss salad and pile on a serving dish. Serve finely chopped watercress separately to sprinkle on salad.
Serves 4

Stilton with port

150 g Stilton or Blaauwkrantz cheese
65 ml thick cream
30 ml port
freshly ground black pepper
4 walnut halves

Mash cheese with a fork, then add cream and port and mix until blended but still rough-textured. Season to taste with pepper and pack into 4 individual moulds. Top each with a walnut half and serve with crackers.
Serves 4

Strawberry tulipes

125 ml castor sugar
125 ml sifted cake flour
1 ml vanilla essence
1-2 egg whites

Filling
250 g fresh ripe strawberries, hulled
50 ml Kirsch (optional)
30 ml sugar
250 ml strawberry sorbet

First make tulipes. Blend castor sugar, flour, vanilla essence well in a food processor or blender. Add 1 egg white and beat, adding more egg white, bit by bit, if mixture seems too thick. Divide mixture into 4 and spread each thinly to the size of a saucer on greased baking sheets. Bake in a pre-heated oven at 200°C for 5-7 minutes or until edges start to darken. Lift with a spatula, remove carefully and place over inverted empty 175 ml yoghurt containers or bowls, pinching sides to form fluted cups. Allow to cool and harden.
   To make filling, toss strawberries in Kirsch and sugar. Just before serving, spoon strawberries into tulipes and top with a scoop of strawberry sorbet. Serve immediately.
Serves 4

Notes
● *Any other seasonal fruit may be used, with an appropriate sorbet for example, melon with melon sorbet.*
● *Tulipes may be made a day in advance and stored in an airtight container until needed. Store them singly, not stacked, in a container to prevent the possibility of their breaking.*
● *Tulipe shapes are available from specialist stores.*

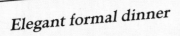

Elegant formal dinner

(Menu for 8)

Baked Brie with pecan nut crust

Poached Cape salmon with seafood hollandaise
and deep-fried celery leaves

Champagne sorbet

Sesame-basted baby chickens

Broccoli ramekins
Boiled new potatoes

Meringue-topped nectarines

Chardonnay or Chenin blanc wine

Baked Brie with pecan nut crust

1 large round Brie cheese
250 ml chopped pecan nuts
100 ml melted butter
butter lettuce leaves

Place Brie on a flat ovenproof dish. Combine nuts with melted butter and use to top cheese. Bake in a pre-heated oven at 200°C for 10 minutes. Place on a dish and serve immediately on butter lettuce leaves.
Serves 4

Note
● *Crust Brie with pecan nut mixture up to 2 hours in advance and bake just before serving.*

Baked Brie with pecan nut crust

Poached Cape salmon with seafood hollandaise and deep-fried celery leaves

15 ml softened butter
4 Cape salmon steaks, each 200-250 g
salt and freshly ground pepper
65 ml very finely chopped onion (±1 large onion)
250 ml dry white wine
50 ml water or fish stock

Deep-fried celery leaves
125 ml soda water
100 ml cake flour
2 ml salt
250 ml tightly packed celery leaves
sunflower oil

Seafood hollandaise
4 egg yolks
20 ml lukewarm water
250 g butter, softened and cubed
2 ml salt
2 ml freshly ground pepper
30 ml lemon juice

First prepare celery leaves. Whisk soda water, flour and salt in a bowl until just combined. Dip celery leaves in mixture and deep-fry batches in hot oil for 30 seconds, turning once. Transfer to absorbent paper to drain, then keep warm, covered.

To prepare fish, spread base of an ovenproof dish with butter, and arrange fish in dish in one layer. Sprinkle with salt, pepper and onion. Pour wine and water or fish stock over and cover with buttered waxproof paper and foil. Poach in a pre-heated oven at 180°C for 10-12 minutes, or until fish just flakes. Transfer fish to a serving platter and keep warm, covered, while making sauce. Strain poaching liquid and set aside.

Make seafood hollandaise by whisking egg yolks with lukewarm water in top of double-boiler. Place over simmering water and beat in butter, bit by bit. Do not allow to boil. Gradually add reserved poaching liquid made up to 200 ml with boiling water, beating constantly. Season with salt, pepper and lemon juice, still beating. Pour over salmon steaks and serve immediately, topped with fried celery leaves.
Serves 4

Champagne sorbet

500 ml water
375 ml sugar
500 ml dry sparkling wine

Heat water and sugar in a medium saucepan over low heat, stirring until sugar dissolves. Increase heat and bring to boil. Reduce heat and simmer for 5 minutes, then cool completely. Refrigerate for 2-3 hours. Stir in sparkling wine and transfer to a rigid freezer container. Freeze until slushy, beat well and return to container. Repeat once, then freeze until firm. Serve scoops of champagne sorbet as a palate cleanser between courses.
Serves 4-6

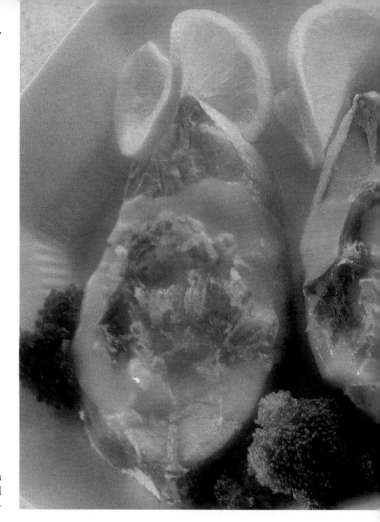

Sesame-basted baby chickens

2 baby chickens, halved

Basting sauce
30 ml dry white wine
30 ml grated lemon rind
30 ml minced fresh ginger
5 ml salt
2 large cloves garlic, crushed
65 ml sunflower oil
45 ml sesame seeds

Place chicken halves in 2 large flat dishes. Combine basting sauce ingredients well and pour over chicken halves. Marinate for 2-3 hours, turning chicken occasionally and spooning basting sauce over. Place chickens in a roasting pan and grill until golden, turning and basting often with basting sauce. Serve immediately with broccoli ramekins* and boiled new potatoes.
Serves 4

Note
● *Chickens may be marinated for up to 5 hours before grilling.*

> **Boiled new potatoes**
> Choose small new potatoes with very thin skins. Scrub well and boil in lightly salted water until tender (about 10 minutes). Drain and serve, in their skins, with butter and finely chopped fresh parsley.

Broccoli ramekins

250 g broccoli, trimmed
15 ml softened butter
15 ml grated Parmesan cheese
50 ml smooth cottage cheese
3 eggs
3 egg yolks
45 ml thick cream or natural yoghurt
10 ml chopped fresh dill
salt and freshly ground pepper
fresh dill sprigs for garnish

Steam broccoli until tender but crisp (5-10 minutes). Drain well and pat dry. Chop coarsely. Grease 4 ramekins, or spray them with non-stick cooking spray, and line bases with greased wax-proof paper. Purée butter, Parmesan cheese, cottage cheese, eggs and egg yolks in a food processor or blender, add cream or yoghurt and purée until smooth. Transfer to a large mixing bowl, fold in broccoli and chopped dill and season to taste with salt and pepper. Pour mixture into ramekins and place in a pan of boiling water, with the water reaching halfway up sides of ramekins. Bake in a pre-heated oven at 180°C for 25-30 minutes, or until set. Unmould onto individual plates, remove waxproof paper and serve garnished with dill sprigs.
Serves 4

Note
● *Prepare mixture for broccoli ramekins up to 2 hours in advance and pour into moulds. Bake just before serving.*

Poached Cape salmon with seafood hollandaise and deep-fried celery leaves

Meringue-topped nectarines

4 ripe nectarines
500 ml unsweetened peach juice
1 stick cinnamon
2 cloves

Meringue topping
3 egg whites at room temperature
pinch salt
pinch cream of tartar
125 ml sugar

Halve, skin and stone nectarines and poach in peach juice with cinnamon and cloves until tender (about 15 minutes). Remove cinnamon and cloves and transfer nectarines and juice to an ovenproof dish.
To make topping, beat egg whites with remaining topping ingredients until stiff peaks form. Spoon over nectarines and brown under a pre-heated grill. Serve immediately.
Serves 4

Note
● *Nectarines may be poached up to 3 hours in advance and kept, covered, at room temperature until needed. Make meringue topping, spoon over nectarines and bake in a pre-heated oven at 180°C for 20-25 minutes.*

Choux puffs with sour cream and caviar filling

Choux pastry
250 ml water
125 ml butter
250 ml cake flour
1 ml salt
4 eggs

Filling
100 ml thick sour cream
125 g smooth cottage cheese
50 g Danish black caviar or lumpfish roe

First make choux puffs. Bring water to boil in a small saucepan. Add butter and stir until melted. Add flour and salt and beat with a wooden spoon until mixture forms a ball. Remove from stove and cool slightly. Add eggs, one at a time, beating constantly. Fill an icing bag with mixture and press out small puffs onto a greased baking sheet. Bake in a pre-heated oven at 200°C for 15 minutes. Lower temperature to 160°C and bake for a further 10 minutes.

Cut a slit in sides of puffs. Combine filling ingredients and use to fill puffs.
Serves 6-8

Notes
• *The choux pastry recipe makes about 50 choux puffs. Store unused puffs in the freezer until needed. To use, thaw and place in a pre-heated oven at 180°C for 3-5 minutes to crisp.*
• *Prepare choux puffs and filling up to 12 hours in advance and assemble just before serving.*

Coffee cheesecake

250 ml crumbled digestive biscuits
250 ml lightly toasted ground almonds
30 ml sugar
75 ml melted butter

Filling
100 ml finely ground coffee beans
125 ml water
500 g smooth cottage cheese
250 ml sugar
100 g dark chocolate, melted with a little milk
300 ml sour cream
4 eggs

First make pie crust. Combine biscuit crumbs, almonds and sugar and mix in butter. Press into base and sides of a 23 cm diameter spring-form cake pan. Refrigerate until firm.

To make filling, combine coffee and water and bring to boil. Strain through a fine-mesh sieve. Combine cottage cheese and sugar until smooth. Add coffee, melted chocolate and sour cream, then beat in eggs and pour mixture into chilled crust. Bake in a pre-heated oven at 180°C for 45 minutes, or until filling is set. Switch oven off and leave cheesecake to cool in oven for 1 hour. Chill well before serving.
Serves 6-8

Note
• *Coffee cheesecake may be made up to 12 hours in advance and refrigerated until needed.*

From left: **Gooseberry tart, choux puffs with sour cream and caviar filling, lacy ginger snaps**

Gooseberry tart

170 g shortcrust pastry*
30 g toasted slivered almonds for decoration

Filling
100 ml castor sugar
juice and grated rind of 1 lemon
2 eggs, separated
100 ml ground almonds
125 ml unsweetened apple juice
250 g ripe Cape gooseberries, hulled

Roll out pastry and use to line a 25 cm diameter spring-form pan. Chill until firm.

Mix 70 ml sugar with grated lemon rind and half the lemon juice. Beat egg yolks and add to lemon mixture with ground almonds. Beat egg whites until stiff and fold into egg yolk mixture. Spoon mixture into prepared pan and bake in pre-heated oven at 190°C for 10 minutes. Reduce temperature to 180°C and bake for a further 15 minutes or until filling is well-risen and lightly browned.

Meanwhile, heat apple juice in a saucepan, add gooseberries and sprinkle with remaining lemon juice and sugar. Cook for 5 minutes, turning gooseberries often. Arrange gooseberries on top of filling and spoon over any syrup that remains. Scatter toasted almond slivers over and serve warm or cold.
Serves 6-8

Notes
• If fresh gooseberries are unavailable, used drained canned ones. Do not poach.
• Gooseberry tart may be made up to 6 hours in advance and refrigerated until needed. If serving warm, reheat at 100°C for 10-15 minutes.

Lacy ginger snaps

65 ml sugar
50 ml butter, cut into pieces
45 ml ginger syrup
85 ml cake flour
1 ml ground ginger

Melt sugar, butter and syrup over medium heat. Stir in flour and ginger, mixing well, and chill for 2 hours. Coat a baking sheet with non-stick cooking spray and drop tablespoonfuls of mixture on it. (Space well, as biscuits spread a lot.) Bake in a pre-heated oven at 180°C for 8 minutes, or until golden. Remove from the oven and allow to stand for 5 minutes, then lift carefully with a spatula and cool on a wire rack.
Serves 6-8

Note
• Ginger snaps may be prepared up to 2 days in advance and stored in an airtight container until needed.

Cool Christmas

(Menu for 6)

Chilled vichyssoise

Smoked turkey

Spicy couscous salad

Julienne vegetables with Caesar vinaigrette

Individual Christmas bombes

Minted Christmas punch

Smoked turkey with spicy couscous
salad and julienne vegetables
with Caesar vinaigrette

Chilled vichyssoise

50 ml butter
500 g leeks, well-washed and sliced
350 g potatoes, sliced
1 stalk celery, sliced
500 ml chicken stock
250 ml cream or natural yoghurt
salt and freshly ground black pepper
2 ml freshly grated nutmeg
finely chopped fresh chives for garnish

Melt butter in a heavy-based saucepan. Add leeks, potatoes and celery and simmer over low heat, covered, until vegetables are slightly yellowed and coated with butter. Add chicken stock, bring to boil and simmer gently for 40 minutes. Cool, purée in a blender or food processor and stir in cream or yoghurt, salt, pepper and nugmeg to taste. Chill for at least 30 minutes before serving, garnished with chives.
Serves 6

Notes
● *For a spicier flavour, 2 ml dill seeds may be added with the stock.*
● *The vichyssoise may be made a day in advance and refrigerated until needed. Stir in a little milk if it thickens too much with chilling.*

Smoked turkey

1 x 2,5 kg turkey, cleaned
15 ml salt
10 ml chicken stock powder
5 ml freshly ground black pepper
5 ml sugar
30 ml flour

Salt turkey inside and out with 7 ml salt. Combine remaining salt, stock powder, pepper, sugar and flour and rub into turkey, inside and out. Sprinkle 30-45 ml untreated oak or other hardwood shavings into a large deep heavy-based saucepan (preferably cast iron) with a tight-fitting lid. Place turkey in a metal container slightly smaller than saucepan and stand on a trivet over wood shavings. Close outer saucepan tightly with lid. Smoke on stove on high for 30 minutes, then reduce heat to medium and smoke turkey for 2 hours. Switch off stove but do not remove saucepan for another 15 minutes. Serve cold, sliced, with cranberry, marula or quince jelly, spicy couscous salad* and crisp steamed julienne vegetables with Caesar vinaigrette*
Serves 6

Notes
● *Do not stuff turkey.*
● *The turkey, couscous salad and vegetables may be served warm, if desired.*
● *Cranberry jelly is available, canned, from supermarkets.*
● *Smoke the turkey a day or two in advance and store in refrigerator until needed.*
● *Leftover turkey can be used in a delicious salad with butter lettuce, sliced kumquats and a sour cream dressing. Sprinkle with nuts if desired.*

Spicy couscous salad

1 x 410 g can plum tomatoes, drained,
    or 500 g fresh tomatoes, skinned
75 ml thinly sliced spring onions (±3-4 spring onions)
15 ml butter
4 ml ground cumin
1 ml ground turmeric
pinch ground cinnamon
65 ml currants
45 ml very finely chopped parsley
200 ml water
300 ml couscous
4 parsley sprigs for garnish

Chop tomatoes and leave to drain through a fine sieve. Sauté spring onion in heated butter in a frying pan over medium heat, stirring, for 1 minute. Stir in cumin, turmeric, cinnamon, tomatoes, currants, chopped parsley and water. Bring to boil, then stir in couscous and let mixture stand, covered, off stove for 5 minutes, or until couscous has absorbed liquid. Leave to cool. Serve garnished with parsley sprigs.
Serves 6

Notes
● *Spicy couscous salad may be prepared a day in advance.*
● *See glossary (page 4) for note on couscous.*

Julienne vegetables with Caesar vinaigrette

6 carrots, cut into julienne strips
6 baby marrows, cut into julienne strips
2 turnips, cut into julienne strips

Caesar vinaigrette
45 ml white wine vinegar
15 ml Dijon mustard
salt and freshly ground pepper
125 ml olive or sunflower oil
5 ml anchovy paste
15 ml capers
1 large egg yolk
125 ml grated Parmesan cheese

Steam vegetables lightly (3-4 minutes) and refresh under cold water. Allow to cool.
   Meanwhile, make vinaigrette. Whisk vinegar, mustard and a pinch of salt in a small bowl. Add oil in a steady stream, whisking, and continue whisking until well-blended. Whisk in anchovy paste, capers, egg yolk and continue whisking to combine well. Whisk in Parmesan cheese and salt and pepper to taste. Serve with julienne vegetables.
Serves 6

Note
● *Instead of the vegetables mentioned above. use baby mealies. young green beans and young cauliflower florets. cut into thin julienne strips.*
● *This dish can be served hot or cold.*

Individual Christmas bombes

2 eggs, separated
60 ml icing sugar, sifted
2 drops vanilla essence
150 ml thick cream

Filling
120 g fruit mincemeat
100 ml chopped mixed nuts
50 ml chopped glacé cherries
50 ml chopped preserved ginger
150 ml thick cream
15 ml icing sugar, sifted
preserved ginger slices for decoration
frosted mint˙ for decoration

Whisk egg whites until stiff. Gradually whisk in icing sugar. Lightly beat egg yolks. Beat vanilla essence and cream separately until mixture forms soft peaks. Fold egg yolks and cream mixture into egg whites. Lightly oil (or spray with non-stick cooking spray) and line bases of 6 tall individual moulds or 175 ml rigid yoghurt containers. Divide mixture among them, spreading it in base and up sides of moulds, leaving a hollow in the centre. Freeze until hard.

To make filling, combine fruit mincemeat, nuts, cherries and ginger. Whip cream until soft peaks form. Sprinkle icing sugar over and fold into cream with chopped fruit. Use to fill hollows in moulds and freeze until both filling and coating are hard. Turn out onto individual plates and decorate each with ginger slices and frosted mint˙. Serve immediately.
Serves 6

Note
• *Make the Christmas bombes up to 2 days in advance and freeze until needed. Thaw slightly in refrigerator before turning out.*

Minted Christmas punch

500 ml unsweetened litchi juice
500 ml unsweetened apple juice
250 ml unsweetened orange juice
250 ml ripe pawpaw, peeled, seeded and cubed
    (± ¼ small pawpaw)
250 ml ripe pineapple, peeled and cubed
    (± ½ small pineapple)
125 ml granadilla pulp (± 3 medium granadillas)
2 x 750 ml bottles dry white wine
1 litre chilled ginger ale or soda water
1 large lemon, thinly sliced
mint sprigs
ice cubes

Combine fruit juices and fruit with wine and chill for at least 1 hour. Add ginger ale or soda water, lemon and mint sprigs just before serving in a bowl over ice.
Serves 6

Notes
• *Make the punch up to 5 hours in advance and chill in the refrigerator until needed.*
• *Make a delicious berry punch with 500 ml unsweetened strawberry juice instead of the litchi juice, 250 ml sliced fresh strawberries instead of the pineapple. Omit the granadillas. Use sparkling wine instead of dry white wine and decorate with halved strawberries instead of mint sprigs.*
• *Serve in frosted glasses as an alternative to the bowl.*

Frosted mint
Dip washed and well-dried mint sprigs first in lightly beaten egg white and then in castor sugar. Place on a baking sheet and bake in a pre-heated oven for 5 minutes at 100°C.

Minted Christmas punch

Tuna mousse with salad and toast fingers

Marinated calamari

2 kg calamari rings
sprigs fresh rosemary for garnish

Marinade
2 cloves garlic, crushed
250 ml olive oil
250 ml white wine vinegar
1 bay leaf
10 whole peppercorns
a few sprigs fresh rosemary
salt and freshly ground black pepper to taste

Parboil calamari rings in lightly salted water to cover for 10 minutes, or until opaque. Drain and place calamari rings in a deep glass bowl. Combine marinade ingredients and pour over calamari. Marinate for at least 24 hours in the refrigerator, turning occasionally. Drain and remove calamari rings from dish, pile on a glass platter and serve, garnished with fresh rosemary sprigs.
Serves 24

Tuna mousse

30 ml gelatine
125 ml cold water
60 ml sugar
10 ml Dijon mustard
10 ml salt
250 ml vinegar
4 egg yolks, lightly beaten
5 ml grated fresh horseradish
30 ml milk
4 x 200 g cans light meat tuna, drained and flaked
500 ml coarsely chopped celery ($\pm$6 large stalks)
250 ml seeded and puréed English cucumber
    (1 small or ½ large)
400 ml whipped cream

Soften gelatine in cold water and set aside. Combine sugar, mustard and salt and place in top of double boiler. Stir in vinegar and egg yolks and cook over boiling water until thick, stirring constantly. Remove from stove and stir in gelatine until dissolved. Combine horseradish and milk and stir into gelatine mixture. Chill until beginning to thicken. Stir in tuna, celery and cucumber, then fold in whipped cream. Pour into two 1,5 litre rinsed moulds or glass dishes, or 24 small moulds, and chill until firm. Serve with salad and toast fingers.
Serves 24

Notes
● *Tuna mousse may also be made in a large (or 2 smaller) rinsed fish-shaped moulds and chilled until set. Turn out onto chilled platters and garnish with dill sprigs.*
● *Tuna mousse may be made up to 1 day in advance and chilled until needed.*

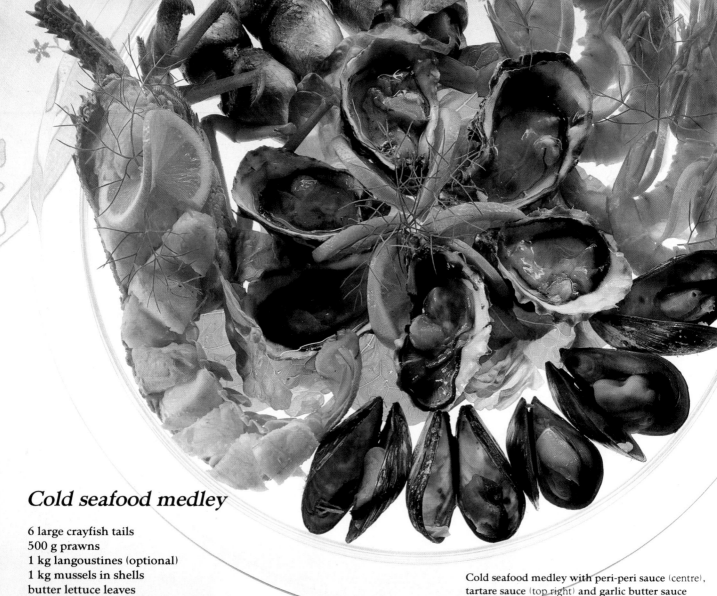

Cold seafood medley

6 large crayfish tails
500 g prawns
1 kg langoustines (optional)
1 kg mussels in shells
butter lettuce leaves
2 kg oysters
500 g smoked eels, cut into chunks, or rollmops
fresh parsley or fennel sprigs for garnish
lemon wedges or halved slices for garnish

Cook crayfish in boiling salted water for 10-15 minutes, or until shells turn bright red. Drain, cool and remove flesh. Chop coarsely into chunks and chill until needed. Cook prawns in boiling salted water to cover for 7-10 minutes, or until bright pink. Drain langoustines in boiling salted water for 10-12 minutes, or until shells turn bright red. Drain and chill until needed. Clean mussels well, scrubbing shells and removing beards. Discard any that are open. Cook in boiling salted water for 10 minutes, or until mussels open. Drain, discarding any that do not open, and chill until needed. Line large flat platters with butter lettuce leaves. Place oysters, preferably on a bed of crushed ice in large bowls, in centre of lettuce-lined platters. Arrange crayfish, prawns, mussels, langoustines and eels or rollmops decoratively around oysters and garnish with parsley sprigs and lemon wedges. Serve peri-peri sauce, garlic butter sauce and tartare sauce separately.
Serves 24

Note
• *Seafood medley may be prepared the day before and chilled, stored in separate containers.*

Cold seafood medley with peri-peri sauce (centre), tartare sauce (top right) and garlic butter sauce

Peri-peri sauce

60 ml butter
30 ml cornflour
1 medium onion, grated
1 small chilli, finely chopped
500 ml fish stock

Melt butter in a saucepan, add cornflour and stir until smooth. Combine onion, chilli and fish stock in a small bowl, add to cornflour mixture and simmer over low heat, stirring, until thickened. Serve hot or cold with seafood.
Makes about 600 ml

Garlic butter sauce

250 g butter
4 cloves garlic, crushed
5 ml salt

Melt butter in a saucepan over low heat. Add garlic and salt, stir to mix well and serve with seafood. Keep warm on a burner.
Makes about 250 ml

Tartare sauce

500 ml mayonnaise
10 finely chopped fresh chives
10 ml finely chopped fresh parsley
10 ml finely chopped capers
2 small pickled gherkins, finely chopped

Combine all ingredients in a small bowl, mix well and refrigerate until needed. Serve with seafood.
Makes 550 ml

Salad choice

Have separate bowls of the following on the table for guests to make up their own salads:

cos lettuce leaves, oak lettuce leaves, finely chopped spinach leaves, bean sprouts, green pepper strips, thin English cucumber slices, onion rings, cherry tomatoes, green and black olives, whole spring onions, whole oyster mushrooms, celery sticks, whole young green beans, lightly steamed baby artichokes, a mixture of chopped fresh herbs.

Serve mustard mayonnaise*, herbed sour cream dressing* and thousand island dressing* separately.

Mustard mayonnaise

500 ml mayonnaise
20-30 ml prepared French mustard

Mix ingredients well and chill until ready to serve.
Makes 500 ml

Herbed sour cream dressing

juice of 2 lemons
10 ml sugar
2 ml salt
freshly ground pepper to taste
2 small cloves garlic, crushed
300 ml sour cream
10 ml chopped fresh dill
10 ml chopped fresh basil
10 ml chopped fresh marjoram

Combine lemon juice, sugar, salt, pepper and garlic in a bowl. Stir in sour cream and herbs, mixing well.
Makes 350 ml

Thousand island dressing

250 ml mayonnaise
125 ml tomato sauce
5 ml Worcestershire sauce
5 ml vinegar
2 ml sugar
1 ml cayenne pepper
2 ml salt
2 ml freshly ground pepper

Combine all ingredients well and serve.
Makes about 400 ml

Crêpes

1 kg cake flour
10 ml salt
10 ml baking powder
8 eggs
2,4 litres milk
250 ml cream
125 ml melted butter or sunflower oil
65 ml brandy

Combine cake flour, salt and baking powder in a bowl. Beat eggs and milk in a separate bowl. Gradually add dry ingredients, beating constantly. Beat in first cream, then melted butter or oil, and brandy. Leave batter to stand for 1 hour before making crêpes. Pre-heat a heavy-based frying pan and grease lightly with oil. Pour a thin layer of batter into pan, tilting it to distribute batter evenly. Bake on one side until lightly browned, about 2 minutes, then turn crêpe over with a spatula and bake for another minute. Turn out onto a plate and keep warm over a saucepan of boiling water or, covered, in the oven at 100 °C. Continue until batter has all been used. Serve with filling of choice: macerated cherries*, nutty ricotta filling* or hazelnut ice*
Make 100 small crêpes

Notes
● *Keep crêpes warm as described above or, stacked on heated plates, on a hot tray.*
● *Crêpes may be made up to a week in advance and frozen, interleaved with waxproof paper or plastic and overwrapped in plastic, until needed. To serve, reheat for 30 seconds on either side in a warm frying pan or in a pre-heated oven at 100 °C for 30 minutes. Keep warm on a hot tray.*

Macerated cherries

1 kg ripe cherries
500 ml Cherry Heering or cherry brandy
65 ml honey

Place cherries in a bowl. Combine liqueur or cherry brandy with heated honey and pour over fruit. Macerate for at least 2 hours at room temperature before serving as a filling for crêpes, with cream or ice cream.
Makes 1 kg

Notes
● *Macerated cherries may be prepared the day before and left to macerate at room temperature until needed.*
● *Other firm berry fruits, such as gooseberries, may be used instead. Substitute gin for Cherry Heering.*

Hazelnut ice

150 g fresh wholewheat breadcrumbs
175 ml ground hazelnuts
350 ml caramel brown sugar
6 egg whites
500 ml Bulgarian yoghurt

Combine breadcrumbs, hazelnuts and 100 g sugar. Spread on a baking sheet and place under a pre-heated grill for 2 minutes, or until golden brown, stirring occasionally. Leave to cool. Whisk egg whites until stiff, then gradually whisk in remaining sugar. Fold in yoghurt and breadcrumb mixture and turn into a rigid freezerproof container. Cover, seal and freeze until firm. Soften in refrigerator for 30 minutes before serving with crêpes.
Makes 1,2 kg

Note
● *Hazelnut ice may be prepared up to a week in advance and kept frozen until 30 minutes before serving. Thaw slightly in refrigerator before use.*

Nutty ricotta filling

500 g ricotta cheese
200 ml slivered almonds
50 ml almond liqueur (optional)
50 ml honey, heated
50 ml finely slivered watermelon preserve

Combine all ingredients well and use as a filling for crêpes.
Makes 650 g

Note
● *Nutty ricotta filling may be prepared up to a day in advance and stored in the refrigerator until needed.*

Crêpes with macerated cherries and cream

INDEX